Acknowledgements

Following the official publication of ITIL, this pocket guide was developed as a concise summary of the ITIL core books, by the authors of the publication "Foundations of ITIL". The text is an update of the ITIL V3 Pocket Guide, that was produced by the editors and reviewers of the ITIL Foundation publication. All members of IPESC, itSMF International's Publication Committee, were invited to participate in the original review, and thirteen itSMF chapters actively participated.

The integrated Review Team was composed of the following:
- Rob van der Burg, Microsoft, Netherlands
- Judith Cremers, Getronics PinkRoccade Educational Services, Netherlands
- Dani Danyluk, Burntsand, itSMF Canada
- John Deland, Sierra Systems, itSMF Canada
- Robert Falkowitz, Concentric Circle Consulting, itSMF Switzerland
- Karen Ferris, itSMF Australia
- Peter van Gijn, Logica, Netherlands
- Kevin Holland, NHS, UK
- Ton van der Hoogen, Tot Z Diensten BV, Netherlands
- Matiss Horodishtiano, Amdocs, itSMF Israel
- Wim Hoving, BHVB, Netherlands
- Brian Johnson, CA, USA
- Steve Mann, Opsys-sm2, itSMF Belgium
- Reiko Morita, Ability InterBusiness Solutions, Inc., Japan
- Ingrid Ouwerkerk, Getronics PinkRoccade Educational Services, Netherlands
- Ton Sleutjes, Capgemini Academy, Netherlands

- Maxime Sottini, iCONS – Innovative Consulting S.r.l., itSMF Italy

The 2011 update of the ITIL pocket guide was reviewed by a smaller section of this Review Team, since it only involved a limited update:
- Rob van der Burg, Microsoft, Netherlands
- John Deland, Sierra Systems, itSMF Canada
- Peter van Gijn, Logica, Netherlands
- Kevin Holland, NHS, UK
- Steve Mann, Opsys-sm2, itSMF Belgium
- Reiko Morita, Ability InterBusiness Solutions, Inc., Japan

All reviewers spent their valuable hours on a detailed review of the text, answering the core question "Is the content a correct reflection of the core content of ITIL, given the limited size of a pocket guide?". Providing several hundreds of valuable improvement issues, they contributed significantly to the quality of this pocket guide, and we thank them for that.

Due to the expert services of the Review Team and the professional support by the editors team, the resulting pocket guide is an excellent entry into the core ITIL books. We are very satisfied with the result, which will be of great value for people wanting to get a first high-level grasp of what ITIL is really all about.

Contents

ITIL® 2011 Edition - A Pocket Guide

Foreword

This concise summary offers a practical introduction to the content of the five ITIL core books. It is based on ITIL 2011 Edition, and explains the structure of the service lifecycle, and the processes and functions of each stage. It also provides support for all the existing users of previous ITIL editions that are looking for a bridge to the new edition.

The 2011 update resolved errors and inconsistencies, and improved clarity, consistency, correctness, and completeness. The Service Strategy book was revised in order to explain the concepts in a clear, concise, and accessible way.

This pocket guide provides the reader with a quick reference to the basic concepts of ITIL. Readers can use the Van Haren Publishing publication "Foundations of ITIL" or the ITIL core volumes (Service Strategy, Service Design, Service Transition, Service Operation and Continual Service Improvement) for more detailed understanding and guidance.

This pocket guide was produced in the same way as other Van Haren Publishing publications: a broad team of expert editors, expert authors and expert reviewers contributed to a comprehensive text, and a great deal of effort was spent on the development and review of the manuscript.

I'm convinced that this pocket guide will provide an excellent reference tool for practitioners, students and others who want a concise summary of the key ITIL concepts.

Jan van Bon

Colophon

Title:	ITIL® 2011 Edition - A Pocket Guide
Author:	Jan van Bon
Publisher:	Van Haren Publishing, Zaltbommel, www.vanharen.net
Design & layout:	CO2 Premedia bv, Amersfoort – NL
ISBN Hard copy:	978 90 8753 676 3
ISBN eBook:	978 90 8753 925 2
ISBN ePUB:	978 90 8753 978 8
Edition:	First edition, first impression, December 2011
	First edition, second impression, March 2012
	First edition, third impression, September 2012
	First edition, fourth impression, April 2013

© 2011 Van Haren Publishing
All rights reserved. No part of this publication may be reproduced in any form by print, photo print, microfilm or any other means without written permission by the publisher.
Although this publication has been composed with much care, neither author, nor editor, nor publisher can accept any liability for damage caused by possible errors and/or incompleteness in this publication.

© Crown copyright 2011. Reproduced under license from The Cabinet Office: cover diagram and diagrams 2.1, 3.1, 3.2, 4.1, 4.3, 4.4, 4.5, 4.6, 4.7, 4.8, 4.9, 5.1, 5.2, 5.3, 5.4, 5.5, 5.6, 5.7, 6.1, 6.2, 6.3, 6.4, 6.5, 6.6, 7.3

TRADEMARK NOTICES

ITIL® is a registered trade mark of the Cabinet Office.
The ITIL Swirl logo™ is a trade mark of the Cabinet Office.
PRINCE2® is a registered trade mark of the Cabinet Office.
COBIT® is a registered trademark of the Information Systems Audit and Control Association (ISACA)/IT Governance Institute (ITGI).
PMBOK® Guide is a registered trademark of the Project Management Institute (PMI).

Licensed Product

ITIL® 2011 Edition - A Pocket Guide

Van Haren
PUBLISHING

1 Introduction

This pocket guide provides the reader with an overview of the
basic concepts of ITIL (ITIL 2011 Edition). Readers can use
the publication "Foundations of ITIL" or the ITIL core volumes
(Service Strategy, Service Design, Service Transition, Service
Operation and Continual Service Improvement) for more
detailed understanding and guidance.

1.1 What is ITIL?

The Information Technology Infrastructure Library™ (ITIL)
offers a systematic approach to the delivery of quality IT services.
ITIL was developed in the 1980s and 1990s by CCTA (Central
Computer and Telecommunications Agency, now the Office
of Government Commerce, OGC), under contract to the UK
Government. Since then, ITIL has provided not only a best
practice based framework, but also an approach and philosophy
shared by the people who work with it in practice. ITIL has now
been updated three times, the first time in 2000-2002 (V2), the
second time in 2007 (V3), and now in 2011. From 2011 onward,
new editions will be named by the year of their release ("ITIL
2011").

Several organizations are involved in the maintenance of the best
practice documentation in ITIL:
- *OGC (Office of Government Commerce)* – Owner of ITIL,
  promoter of best practices in numerous areas including IT
  service management.
- *itSMF (IT Service Management Forum)* – A global,
  independent, internationally recognized not-for-profit
  organization dedicated to support the development of IT
  service management, e.g. through publications in the ITSM

Library series. It consists of a growing number of national chapters (40+), with itSMF International as the controlling body.

- *APM Group* – In 2006, OGC contracted the management of ITIL rights, the certification of ITIL exams and accreditation of training organizations to the APM Group (APMG), a commercial organization. APMG defines the certification and accreditation schemes for the ITIL exams, and publishes the associated certification system.
- *Examination institutes* – To support the world-wide delivery of the ITIL exams, APMG has accredited a number of exam bodies: BCS-ISEB, CERT-IT, CSME, DANSK IT, DF Certifiering AB, EXIN, Loyalist Certification Services, PEOPLECERT Group, and TÜV SÜD Akademie. See www.itil-officialsite.com for recent information.

1.2 Why is ITIL successful?

ITIL combines a number of characteristics that makes it a valuable and effective instrument, aiming at that one goal that really counts: delivering value to the business. It is vendor-neutral, making sure it is applicable to any IT organization, whatever products are used. It is non-prescriptive, making sure it can be adopted and adapted in organizations in any line of business, be it public or private, internal or external, small or large. And finally, it is best practice: it represents the lessons of the best performing organizations in the IT service business today.

1.3 ITIL exams

In 2007 the accreditor (APM Group) launched a new qualification scheme for ITIL, based on ITIL V3. The ITIL V2 certification ceased in mid 2011. Candidates who hold existing

ITIL V3 certification will not need to become re-certified with the ITIL 2011 update. The accreditor has no plans to introduce any bridging examinations for the update, as the core ITIL process areas and principles have not changed significantly.

ITIL V2 had qualifications on three levels:
- *Foundation Certificate* in IT Service Management
- *Practitioner's Certificate* in IT Service Management
- *Manager's Certificate* in IT Service Management

The ITIL V2 exams proved to be a great success. Up to 2000, some 60,000 certificates had been issued. In the following years the numbers rocketed, and by 2006 they had broken the 500,000 mark.

For ITIL V3 a new system of qualifications was set up. This also applies to the ITIL 2011 edition. There are four qualification levels:
- Foundation Level
- Intermediate Level (Lifecycle Stream & Capability Stream)
- ITIL Expert Level
- ITIL Master Qualification

Each of the service lifecycle stages requires appropriate skills and experience of people involved, so they can work effectively and efficiently throughout the lifecycle. Core skills, attributes and competencies include business awareness, a basic understanding of what IT can contribute to the business, customer service skills, and the ability to work with best practice and policies. The Skills Framework for the Information Age (SFIA) is often used as a common reference model for IT organizations. SFIA defines a standardized skills structure for tasks and core competencies.

For more information about the ITIL qualification scheme, see
http://www.itil-officialsite.com/qualifications. More information
on SFIA can be found at www.sfia.org.uk

1.4   Structure of this pocket guide

Chapter 2 introduces the service lifecycle, in the context of IT
service management principles. It discusses the functions and
processes that are referred to in each of the lifecycle stages. It
provides general information on principles of processes, teams,
roles, functions, positions, tools, and other elements of interest.
It also shows how the processes, the common activities, and the
functions are clustered in the 5 ITIL core books.

In Chapters 3 to 7, each of the stages in the service lifecycle is
discussed in detail, following a standardized structure: service
strategy, service design, service transition, service operation and
continual service improvement. For each process and function,
the following information is provided:
• introduction
• basic concepts
• activities

1.5   How to use this pocket guide

Readers who are primarily interested in getting a quick
understanding of the service lifecycle can focus on the
introduction chapters of the pocket guide, and pick whatever they
need on specific functions and processes from the other chapters.

2 Introduction to the service lifecycle

2.1 Definition of service management

ITIL is presented as "*best practice*". Best practice is an approach or method that has been proven in practice. Best practices can be a solid backing for organizations that want to improve their IT services.

The ITIL service lifecycle is based on ITIL's core concept of "service management" and the related concepts "service" and "value". These core terms in service management are explained as follows:

- *Service management* – A set of specialized organizational capabilities for providing value to customers in the form of services.
- *Service* – A means of delivering value to customers by facilitating outcomes the customers want to achieve without the ownership of specific costs or risks. Outcomes are possible from the performance of tasks and they are limited by a number of constraints. Services enhance performance and reduce the pressure of constraints. This increases the chances of the desired outcomes being realized.
- *Value* – Value is the core of the service concept. From the customer's perspective, value consists of two core components: utility and warranty. Utility is what the customer receives, and warranty is how it is provided. The concepts "utility" and "warranty" are described in the Section on service strategy.

2.2 Internal and external customers

Internal customers are people or departments who are part of the same organization as the service provider. These customers may be business units, departments, teams, or any other type of organizational unit.

External customers are people who are not employed by the organization, or organizations that are separate legal entities. The agreements between a service provider and external customers are legally binding contracts. External customers pay with 'real money' (or goods).

Both internal and external customers must be provided with the agreed level of service, with the same levels of customer service.

2.3 Internal and external services

There also are internal and external services. Internal services are delivered to customers in the same organization. External services are delivered to external customers.

2.4 Overview of the service lifecycle

ITIL approaches service management from the lifecycle aspect of a service. The service lifecycle is an organizational model that provides insight into:

- the way service management is structured
- the way the various lifecycle components are linked to each other
- the impact that changes in one component will have on other components and on the entire lifecycle system.

Thus, ITIL focuses on the service lifecycle, and the way service management components are linked. Processes and functions are also discussed in the lifecycle stages.

The service lifecycle consists of five stages. Each volume of the new core ITIL volumes describes one of these stages. The related processes are described in detail in the stage where they have the strongest association.

The five stages (domains of the core books) are:

1. *Service strategy* – the stage that defines the requirements for a service provider to be able to support the business requirements. It describes the strategy of delivering and managing services to the customer, in the perspective of added value to the customer's business.

2. *Service design* – the stage where services are designed, and planned for introduction into the service delivery environment. It includes several practices, making sure that services are designed with the business objectives in mind.

3. *Service transition* – following up on service strategy and service design stages of the lifecycle, the activities in this stage ensure that service releases are deployed successfully into supported environments, and that new, modified or retired services meet the expectations of the business, while controlling the risks of failure and subsequent disruption.

4. *Service operation* – this is the stage where the service provider coordinates and carries out the activities and processes required to deliver and manage services at agreed levels to business users and customers.

5. *Continual service improvement* – the fifth stage describes best practice for achieving incremental and large-scale improvements in service quality, operational efficiency and business continuity, and for ensuring that the service portfolio continues to be aligned to business needs.

Service strategy is the axis of the service lifecycle (Figure 2.1) that drives all other stages; it is the stage of policymaking and setting objectives. The service design, service transition and service operation stages are guided by this strategy; their continual theme is adjustment and change. The continual service improvement stage stands for learning and improving, and embraces all other lifecycle stages. This stage initiates improvement programs and projects, and prioritizes them based on the strategic objectives of the organization.

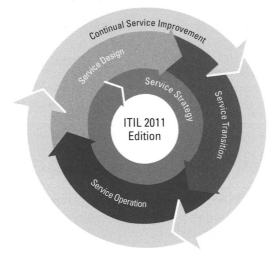

Figure 2.1 The service lifecycle
Source: the Cabinet Office

2.5 Functions and processes

Each of the lifecycles describes a number of processes and a number of functions. Processes and functions are defined as follows:

- *Process* – A structured set of activities designed to accomplish a defined objective. Processes have inputs and outputs, result in a goal-oriented change, and utilize feedback for self-enhancing and self-corrective actions. Processes are measurable, provide results to customers or stakeholders, are continual and iterative and are always originating from a certain event. Processes can run through several organizational units. An example of a process is change management.

- *Function* – A team or group of people and the tools they use to carry out one or more processes or activities, specialized in fulfilling a specified type of work, and responsible for specific end results. Functions have their own practices and their own knowledge body. Functions can make use of various processes. An example of a function is a service desk. (Note: "function" can also mean "functionality", "functioning", or "job".)

Processes are often described using procedures and work instructions:

- A *procedure* is a specified way to carry out an activity or a process. A procedure describes the "how", and can also describe "who" executes the activities. A procedure may include stages from different processes. Procedures will vary depending on the organization.
- A set of *work instructions* defines how one or more activities in a procedure should be executed in detail, using technology or other resources.

2.6 Organizational structure

When setting up an organization, positions and roles are also used, in addition to the various groups (teams, departments, divisions):

- *Roles* are sets of responsibilities, activities and authorities granted to a person or team. One person or team may have

multiple roles; for example, the roles of configuration manager and change manager may be carried out by one person.
- *Job positions* are traditionally recognized as tasks and responsibilities that are assigned to a specific person. A person in a particular position has a clearly defined package of tasks and responsibilities which may include various roles. Positions can also be more broadly defined as a logical concept that refers to the people and automated measures that carry out a clearly defined process, an activity or a combination of processes or activities. Individuals and roles have an N:N relationship (many-to-many).

We can study each process separately to optimize its quality:
- The *process owner* is responsible for the process results.
- The *process manager* is responsible for the realization and structure of the process, and reports to the process owner.
- The *process practitioners* are responsible for defined activities, and these activities are reported to the process manager.

The management of the organization can provide control on the basis of data from each process. In most cases, the relevant performance indicators and standards will already be agreed upon, and the process manager can take day-to-day control of the process. The process owner will assess the results based on performance indicators and check whether the results meet the agreed standard. Without clear indicators, it would be difficult for a process owner to determine whether the process is under control, and if planned improvements are being implemented.

When setting up a service or a process, it is imperative that all roles are clearly defined and that it is clear who does what. For this purpose, a responsibility model like RACI can be used.

RACI provides an 'authority matrix' to define the roles and responsibilities in relation to processes and activities.

RACI is an acronym for the four main roles:

- *Responsible* – The person or people responsible for correct execution – for getting the job done.
- *Accountable* – The person who has ownership of quality and the end result. Only one person can be accountable for each task.
- *Consulted* – The people who are consulted and whose opinions are sought. They have involvement through input of knowledge and information.
- *Informed* – The people who are kept up to date on progress. They receive information about process execution and quality.

People, process, products and partners (the four Ps) provide the main "machinery" of any organization, but they only work well if the machine is oiled: *communication* is an essential element in any organization. If the people do not know about the processes or use the wrong instructions or tools, the outputs may not be as anticipated. Formal structures on communication include:

- *Reporting* – Internal and external reporting, aimed at management or customers, project progress reports, alerts.
- *Meetings* – Formal project meetings, regular meetings with specific targets.
- *Online facilities* – Email systems, chat rooms, pagers, groupware, document sharing systems, messenger facilities, teleconferencing and virtual meeting facilities.
- *Notice boards* – Near the coffee maker, at the entrance of the building, in the company restaurant.

It is recommended that a common understanding of processes, projects, programs, and even portfolios is created. The following definitions may be used:

- *Process* – A process is a structured set of activities designed to accomplish a defined objective.
- *Project* – A project is a temporary organization, with people and other assets required to achieve an objective.
- *Program* – A program consists of a number of projects and activities that are planned and managed together to achieve an overall set of related objectives.
- *Portfolio* – A portfolio is a set of projects and/or programs, which are not necessarily related, brought together for the sake of control, coordination and optimization of the portfolio in its totality. NB: A service portfolio is the complete set of services that are managed by a service provider.

2.7   ITIL lifecycle clustering

ITIL contains five core books – one for each stage of the lifecycle. Each of the five lifecycle stages describes processes, functions and "miscellaneous activities". This lifecycle classification represents another dimension of the process structure, which describes the service provider's operating method. As such, a process generally occurs in multiple stages.

The detailed description of a process or function is included in just one of the five books, even if the process is also relevant in other stages (books). In this case, the book in which the process or function makes its main contribution to the lifecycle is selected.

The processes, activities, and functions described in the lifecycle stages are listed in ITIL order below:

Service strategy processes:
- Strategy management for IT services
- Service portfolio management
- Financial management for IT services
- Demand management
- Business relationship management.

Service design processes:
- Design coordination
- Service catalogue management
- Service level management
- Availability management
- Capacity management
- IT service continuity management (ITSCM)
- Information security management
- Supplier management.

Service transition processes:
- Transition planning and support
- Change management
- Service asset and configuration management
- Release and deployment management
- Service validation and testing
- Change evaluation
- Knowledge management.

Service operation processes:
- Event management
- Incident management
- Request fulfillment
- Problem management
- Access management.

Continual service improvement processes:
- The seven-step improvement process (CSI improvement process).

Service design technology-related activities:
- Requirements engineering
- Management of data and information
- Management of applications.

Service operation common activities:
- Monitoring and control
- IT operations
- Server and mainframe management and support
- Network management
- Storage and archive
- Database administration
- Directory services management
- Desktop and mobile device support
- Middleware management
- Internet/web management
- Facilities and data centre management.

Service operation functions:
- Service desk
- Technical management
- IT operations management
- Application management.

Note: all together there are more than 26 processes in ITIL, since some of the processes, like financial management for IT services, are composed of sub-processes.

The next chapters show these processes, activities, and functions in the various lifecycle stages.

2.8 The process model and the characteristics of processes

A process is a structured set of activities designed to accomplish a specific objective. A process takes one or more defined inputs and turns them into defined outputs. Process characteristics include:

- *Measurability* – We are able to measure the process in a relevant manner. It is performance-driven. Managers want to measure cost, quality and other variables while practitioners are concerned with duration and productivity.
- *Specific results* – The reason a process exists is to deliver a specific result. This result must be individually identifiable and countable.
- *Customers* – Every process delivers its primary results to a customer or stakeholder. Customers may be internal or external to the organization, but the process must meet their expectations.
- *Responsiveness to specific triggers* – While a process may be ongoing or iterative, it should be traceable to a specific trigger.

A process is organized around a set of objectives. The main outputs from the process should be driven by the objectives and should include process measurements (metrics), reports and process improvement.

If the process output conforms to the operational norm, the process can be considered effective. If the process consumes a minimum use of resources, the process can also be considered efficient. Processes should be documented and controlled.

2.9 Key concepts

The ITIL Glossary specifies the terms used in ITIL. These include the following key concepts.

Alert

A notification that a threshold has been reached, something has changed, or a failure has occurred. Alerts are often created and managed by system management tools and are managed by the event management process.

Assets, resources and capabilities

An asset is any resource or capability. The assets of a service provider include anything that could contribute to the delivery of a service. Assets can be one of the following types: management, organization, process, knowledge, people, information, applications, infrastructure or financial capital.

A customer asset is any resource or capability used by a customer to achieve a business outcome. A service asset is any resource or capability used by a service provider to deliver services to a customer. Resource is a generic term that includes IT infrastructure, people, money or anything else that might help to deliver an IT service. Resources are considered to be assets of an organization.

Capability is the ability of an organization, person, process, application, IT service or other configuration item to carry out an activity. Capabilities are intangible assets of an organization.

Business case

Justification for a significant item of expenditure. The business case includes information about costs, benefits, options, issues, risks and possible problems.

Change
The addition, modification or removal of anything that could have an effect on IT services. The scope should include changes to all architectures, processes, tools, metrics and documentation, as well as changes to IT services and other configuration items.

Change proposals and change requests
A request for change (RFC) is a formal proposal for a change to be made. It includes details of the proposed change, and may be recorded on paper or electronically. The term is often misused to mean a change record, or the change itself.

In situations where significant changes are requested, or new services are introduced, a change proposal may precede the actual change request. The change proposal then is a document that includes a high level description of a potential service introduction or significant change, along with a corresponding business case and an expected implementation schedule. Change proposals are normally created by the service portfolio management process and are passed to change management for authorization. Change management will review the potential impact on other services, on shared resources, and on the overall change schedule. Once the change proposal has been authorized, service portfolio management will charter the service, and RFCs will be used to introduce the actual change.

Change types
There are three different types of service change:
- A standard change is a pre-authorized change that is low risk, relatively common and follows a procedure or work instruction.

- An emergency change is a change that must be implemented as soon as possible, for example to resolve a major incident or implement a security patch.
- A normal change is any service change that is not a standard change nor an emergency change.

Communication in service operation

In service operation, where the actual services are delivered, good communication is needed with other IT teams and departments, with users and internal customers, and between the service operation teams and departments themselves. Issues can often be prevented or mitigated with appropriate communication. The communication can relate to all kinds of operational communication, between shifts, on performance, related to changes, exceptions, emergencies, et cetera. It can take place in formal meetings, through social media, or in any other format, as determined by the organization's culture and standard operating procedures.

Configuration item (CI)

Any component or other service asset that needs to be managed in order to deliver an IT service. Configuration items are under the control of change management. They typically include IT services, hardware, software, buildings, people and formal documentation such as process documentation and service level agreements.

Configuration management system (CMS)

A set of tools, data and information that is used to support service asset and configuration management. The CMS is part of an overall service knowledge management system and includes tools for collecting, storing, managing, updating, analyzing and presenting data about all configuration items and their relationships. The CMS may also include information about incidents, problems, known errors, changes and releases. The CMS is maintained by service asset and configuration management and is used by all IT service management processes.

CSI register
A database or structured document used to record and manage improvement opportunities throughout their lifecycle.

Customers and users
In service management, customers and users represent two different levels. A customer is someone who buys goods or services. The customer of an IT service provider is the person or group who defines and agrees the service level targets. There can be one or many users in a customer organization. A user is a person who uses the IT service on a day-to-day basis. Users are distinct from customers, as some customers do not use the IT service directly.

Definitive media library (DML)
One or more locations in which the definitive and authorized versions of all software configuration items are securely stored. The definitive media library may also contain associated configuration items such as licenses and documentation. It is a single logical storage area even if there are multiple locations. The definitive media library is controlled by service asset and configuration management and is recorded in the configuration management system.

Deming Cycle (plan, do, check, act)

A four stage cycle for process improvement, attributed to W. Edwards Deming. The Deming Cycle is also called Plan-Do-Check-Act:

- *Plan* – design or revise processes that support the IT services
- *Do* – implement the plan and manage the processes
- *Check* – measure the processes and IT services, compare with objectives and produce reports
- *Act* – plan and implement changes to improve the processes.

Event

A change of state that has significance for the management of an IT service or other configuration item. The term is also used to mean an alert or notification created by any IT service, configuration item or monitoring tool. Events typically require IT operations personnel to take actions, and often lead to incidents being logged.

Governance

Governance ensures that policies and strategy are actually implemented, and that required processes are correctly followed. Governance includes defining roles and responsibilities, measuring and reporting, and taking actions to resolve any issues identified.

Impact, urgency and priority

Not all calls and issues in service delivery can be handled at the same time, as resources are limited. The relative importance of an incident, problem or change is determined by its priority. A priority is based on impact and urgency, and is used to identify required times for actions to be taken. For example, the service level agreement may state that Priority 2 incidents must be resolved within 12 hours. Impact is a measure of the effect of an incident, problem or change on business processes. Impact is often based on how service levels will be affected. Impact and urgency are used to assign priority. Urgency is a measure of how long it will be until an incident, problem or change has a significant impact on the business. For example, a high-impact incident may have low urgency if the impact will not affect the business until the end of the financial year. Impact and urgency are used to assign priority.

Incident
An unplanned interruption to an IT service or reduction in the quality of an IT service. Failure of a configuration item that has not yet affected service is also an incident – for example, failure of one disk from a mirror set.

Known error
A known error is a problem that has a documented root cause and a workaround. Known errors are created and managed throughout their lifecycle by problem management. Known errors may also be identified by development or suppliers.

Known error database (KEDB)
A database containing all known error records. This database is created by problem management and used by incident and problem management. The known error database may be part of the configuration management system, or may be stored elsewhere in the service knowledge management system.

Operational level agreement (OLA)
An agreement between an IT service provider and another part of the same organization. It supports the IT service provider's

delivery of IT services to customers and defines the goods or services to be provided and the responsibilities of both parties. For example, there could be an operational level agreement:
- between the IT service provider and a procurement department to obtain hardware in agreed times
- between the service desk and a support group to provide incident resolution in agreed times.

Patterns of business activity (PBA)
A workload profile of one or more business activities. Patterns of business activity are used to help the IT service provider understand and plan for different levels of business activity.

Problem
A cause of one or more incidents. The cause is not usually known at the time a problem record is created, and the problem management process is responsible for further investigation.

Release policy
A release policy defines the criteria, roles, responsibilities, aggregating approach, and techniques to be used for managing aggregated changes as a release. A release policy is applied to each service, and is agreed with the business and all relevant parties.

Risk management
The process responsible for identifying, assessing and controlling risks. Risk management is also sometimes used to refer to the second part of the overall process after risks have been identified and assessed, as in 'risk assessment and management'. This process is not described in detail within the core ITIL publications.

Service catalogue
A database or structured document with information about all live IT services, including those available for deployment. The service catalogue is part of the service portfolio and contains information about two types of IT service: customer-facing services that are visible to the business; and supporting services required by the service provider to deliver customer-facing services.

Service design package (SDP)
Document(s) defining all aspects of an IT service and its requirements through each stage of its lifecycle. A service design package is produced for each new IT service, major change or IT service retirement.

Service knowledge management system (SKMS)
A set of tools and databases that is used to manage knowledge, information and data. The service knowledge management system includes the configuration management system, as well as other databases and information systems. The service knowledge management system includes tools for collecting, storing, managing, updating, analyzing and presenting all the knowledge, information and data that an IT service provider will need to manage the full lifecycle of IT services.

Service level agreement (SLA)
An agreement between an IT service provider and a customer. An SLA describes the IT service, documents service level targets, and specifies the responsibilities of the IT service provider and the customer. A single agreement may cover multiple IT services or multiple customers.

Service portfolio
The complete set of services that is managed by a service provider. The service portfolio is used to manage the entire lifecycle of all services, and includes three categories: service pipeline (proposed or in development), service catalogue (live or available for deployment), and retired services.

Service provider
An organization supplying services to one or more internal customers or external customers. Service provider is often used as an abbreviation for IT service provider.

Service request
A formal request from a user for something to be provided – for example, a request for information or advice; to reset a password; or to install a workstation for a new user. Service requests are managed by the request fulfillment process, usually in conjunction with the service desk. Service requests may be linked to a request for change as part of fulfilling the request.

Service types
All services can be classified in terms of how they relate to one another and their customers. There are three types of IT service:
- Core services deliver the basic outcomes desired by one or more customers.
- Enabling services, that are needed in order for a core service to be delivered.
- Enhancing services, that are added to a core service to make it more exciting or enticing to the customer.

Each of these types can be used as a supporting service, an internal customer-facing service, or an external customer-facing service.

Supplier
A third party responsible for supplying goods or services that are required to deliver IT services. Examples of suppliers include commodity hardware and software vendors, network and telecom providers, and outsourcing organizations.

Underpinning contract
A contract between an IT service provider and a third party. The third party provides goods or services that support delivery of an IT service to a customer. The underpinning contract defines targets and responsibilities that are required to meet agreed service level targets in one or more service level agreements.

Utility and warranty
The functionality offered by a product or service to meet a particular need. Utility can be summarized as 'what the service does', and can be used to determine whether a service is able to meet its required outcomes, or is 'fit for purpose'. Warranty can be summarized as 'how the service is delivered', and can be used to determine whether a service is 'fit for use'. The business value of an IT service is created by the combination of utility and warranty.

Workaround
A measure to reduce or eliminate the impact of an incident or problem for which a full resolution is not yet available – for example, by restarting a failed configuration item. Workarounds for problems are documented in known error records. Workarounds for incidents that do not have associated problem records are documented in the incident record.

3 Lifecycle stage: service strategy

3.1 Introduction

In this section, the axis (principal line of development, movement, direction, reference point) of the lifecycle is introduced. As the axis of the lifecycle, service strategy delivers guidance with designing, developing and implementing service management as a strategic asset. Service strategy is critical in the context of all processes along the ITIL service lifecycle.

The mission of the service strategy stage is to develop the capacity to achieve and maintain a strategic advantage.

The development and application of service strategy requires constant revision, just as in all other components of the cycle.

3.2 Basic concepts

To formulate the strategy, Mintzberg's four Ps are a good starting point (Mintzberg, 1994):

- *Perspective* – Have a clear vision and focus.
- *Position* – Take a clearly defined stance.
- *Plan* – Form a precise notion of how the organization should develop itself.
- *Pattern* – Maintain consistency in decisions and actions.

Value creation is a combination of the effects of utility and warranty. Both are necessary for the creation of value for the customer. For customers, the positive effect is the "utility" of a service; the insurance of this positive effect is the "warranty":

- *Utility – fitness for purpose.* Functionality offered by a product or service to meet a particular need. Utility is often summarized as "what it does".
- *Warranty – fitness for use.* A promise or guarantee that a product or service will meet its agreed requirements. The availability, capacity, continuity and information security necessary to meet the customers' requirements.

The *value networks* are defined as follows: "A value network is a web of relationships that generate both tangible and intangible value through complex and dynamic exchanges between two or more organizations."

Resources and capabilities are the *service assets* of a service provider. Organizations use them to create value in the form of goods and services.

- *Resources* – Resources include IT Infrastructure, people, money or anything else that might help to deliver an IT service. Resources comprise the direct input for the production.
- *Capabilities* – Capabilities are used to develop, implement and coordinate the production. Service providers must develop distinctive capabilities in order to maintain services that are difficult to duplicate by the competition. Service providers must also invest substantially in education and training.

Service providers are organizations that supply services to one or more internal or external customers. Three different types of service providers are distinguished:

- *Type I: Internal service provider* – An internal service provider that is embedded within a business unit (BU). There may be several type I service providers within an organization.

- *Type II: Shared services unit* – An internal service provider that provides shared IT services to more than one business unit.
- *Type III: External service provider* – A service provider that provides IT services to external customers.

The *service portfolio* represents the opportunities and readiness of a service provider to serve the customers and the market space. The service portfolio can be divided into three subsets of services: *service catalogue*, *service pipeline,* and *retired services.*

3.3 Processes and other activities

This section explains the processes and activities of service strategy.

The service strategy processes:
- *Strategy management for IT services* – The process responsible for developing and maintaining IT strategies from a business point of view. It includes a specification of the type of services to be delivered, the customers of the services, and the overall business outcomes to be achieved through these services.
- *Service portfolio management (SPM)* – Method to manage all service management investments in terms of business value. The objective of SPM is to achieve maximum value creation while at the same time managing the risks and costs.
- *Financial management* – An integral component of service management. It anticipates the essential management information in financial terms that is required for the guarantee of efficient and cost-effective service delivery.
- *Demand management* – An essential aspect of service management in which offer and demand are harmonized. The goal of demand management is to predict, as accurately

as possible, the purchase of products and, where possible, to
balance the demand with the resources.
- *Business relationship management* – The process that is
responsible for the alignment between services and business
needs. It helps to identify and understand customer needs and
to ensure that the service provider is capable of delivering the
required services.

3.4   Strategy management for IT services

Introduction
Strategy management for IT services is the process that ensures
that the IT strategy is defined, maintained and achieves its
purpose. It is defined by business strategy.
The purpose of a service strategy is to articulate how a service
provider will enable an organization to achieve its business
outcomes; it establishes the criteria and mechanisms to decide
which services will be best suited to meet the business outcomes
and the most effective and efficient way to manage these services.

Basic concepts
By developing and maintaining a clear service strategy, an
organization can set clear objectives, and control whether
objectives are met. The strategy is the base for all tactical plans,
which in turn determine the service operation. Having an agreed
service strategy in place ensures that all involved parties have the
same understanding on directions, options, and choices made for
the organization's development.

Activities
The strategy management for IT services process analyses the
provider's internal and external environment, to identify and

manage opportunities and constraints for service delivery. It develops a clear vision and mission statement on the service provider's position and the decisions on services that will be delivered.

The strategic plans are documented and distributed to all relevant stakeholders, and reviewed regularly to ensure that they keep pace with changes to the internal and external environments.

Once the strategy has been set, it is ensured that these are translated into tactical and operational plans for each organizational unit that is expected to deliver on the strategy.

3.5 Service portfolio management

Introduction

A service portfolio describes the services of a provider in terms of business value. It is a dynamic method used to govern investments in service management across the enterprise, in terms of financial values. With service portfolio management (SPM), managers are able to assess the quality requirements and accompanying costs.

The goal of service portfolio management is to realize maximum value while managing risks and costs.

Basic concepts

By functioning as the basis of the decision framework, the service portfolio helps to answer the following strategic questions:

- Why should a client buy these services?
- Why should a client buy these services from us?
- What are the price and charge back models?

- What are our strong and weak points, our priorities and our risks?
- How should our resources and capabilities be allocated?

With an efficient portfolio having optimal return on investment (ROI) and risk levels, an organization can maximize the value realization on its constrained and limited resources and capabilities.

Service owners play an important role in the SPM. They are responsible for managing services as products during the entire lifecycle. Service owners coordinate and focus the organization and own the service information in the service catalogue. They work closely together with the business relationship managers (BRMs), who coordinate and focus on the client portfolio. In essence, SPM is a governance method.

The service portfolio covers three subsets of services:
- *Service catalogue* – That part of the service portfolio that is visible to customers. The service catalogue is an essential strategy tool because it can be viewed as the virtual projection of the actual and available capabilities of the service provider.
- *Service pipeline* – Consists of all services that are either under consideration or in development for a specific market or customer. These services are to be applied in the production stage via the service transition stage. The pipeline represents the growth and strategic anticipation for the future.
- *Retired services* – Services that are phased out or withdrawn. The phasing out of services is a component of service transition and is necessary to guarantee that all agreements with customers will be kept.

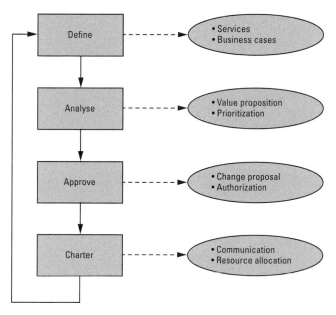

Figure 3.1 Service portfolio management
Source: the Cabinet Office

Activities

SPM is a dynamic and continuous process that entails the following work methods (see also Figure 3.1):

- *Define* – Making an inventory of services, business cases and validating the portfolio data; start with collecting information on all existing and proposed services in order to determine the costs of the existing portfolio; the cyclic nature of the SPM process signifies that this stage does not only make an inventory of the services, but also validates the data over and over again; each service in the portfolio should have a business case.

- *Analyze* – Maximizing the portfolio value, tuning, prioritizing and balancing supply and demand; in this stage, the strategic goals are given a concrete form. Start with a series of top/down questions such as: What are the long-term goals of the service organization? Which services are required to realize these goals? Which capabilities and resources are necessary to attain these services? The answers to these questions form the basis of the analysis, but also determine the desired result of SPM. Service investments must be subdivided into three strategic categories:
  - *Run the Business* – RTB investments concentrate on maintaining the service production.
  - *Grow the Business* – GTB investments are intended to expand the scope of services.
  - *Transform the Business* – TTB investments are meant to move into new market spaces.
- *Approve* – Finishing the proposed portfolio, authorizing services and resources and making decisions for the future. There are six different outcomes: retain, replace, rationalize, refactor, renew and retire.
- *Charter* – Communicating decisions, allocating resources and chartering services. Start with a list of decisions and action items and communicate these clearly and unambiguously to the organization. Decisions must be in tune with the budget decisions and financial plans. New services proceed to the services design stage and existing services are renewed in the service catalogue.

3.6 Financial management for IT services

Introduction

Financial management for IT services is the process responsible for managing an IT service provider's budgeting, accounting and charging requirements. It is also the process that is used to quantify the value that IT services contribute to the business.

Financial management is an integrated component of service management. It provides vital information for management to guarantee efficient and cost-effective service delivery. If strictly implemented, financial management generates meaningful and critical data on performance. It is also able to answer important organizational issues, such as:
- Does our differentiation strategy result in higher profits and revenue, reduced costs or increased coverage?
- Which services cost most and why?
- Where are our greatest inefficiencies?

Financial management ensures that the charges for IT services are transparent via the service catalogue and that the business understands them. The benefits are:
- improved decision-making
- inputs for service portfolio management
- financial compliance and control
- operational control
- value capture and creation.

Basic concepts

An organization needs to decide how it will position the IT department in terms of financial management: will IT be a profit or a cost centre?

- *Cost centre* – IT is positioned as a department to which costs are assigned, but which does not charge for services provided. It should take responsibility for the spending of the allocated budget, and to account for the money spent, from a business point of view. Cost awareness can be stimulated, without the overheads of billing, but the organization is limited in its ability to manage the IT department financially.
- *Profit centre* – IT is positioned as a department that charges for the services it provides to the rest of the organization. As a profit centre IT has more independent control over its financial assets and undertakings. Charging other departments can support cost awareness, demonstrating the value that IT delivers to the rest of the organization.

It is also important to determine the funding of the IT department, the sourcing and allocation of money for the department's spending. Funding can be external or internal:

- *External funding* – Comes from revenue that is received from selling services to external customers.
- *Internal funding* – Comes from other business units inside the same organization.

Funding models help to define how and when the IT service provider will be funded:

- *Rolling plan funding* – A rolling plan is a plan for a fixed number of cycles (months, years). At the end of the first cycle, the plan is extended by one more cycle. Funding requirements can be adjusted for each cycle. Often used for projects.
- *Trigger-based funding* – In this model a plan is initiated and funding is provided when a specific situation or event occurs. The trigger can relate to a change, to a capacity requirement, or any other ad hoc situation.

- *Zero-based funding* – Most internal service providers are funded using this model, since it is based on ensuring that IT breaks even. In this model IT is allowed to spend up to the agreed budget amount, or get special approval to spend over the amount, and at the end of the financial period (monthly, quarterly or annually) the money is recovered from the other business units through cost transfers. This equates to funding only the actual costs to deliver the IT services.

Activities

Financial management consists of three main processes:

- *Budgeting* – The activity of predicting and controlling the spending of money. Budgeting creates clear images of the income and expenditure of money in the organization. Budgets are negotiated and set on a periodical base, and monitored continually.
- *Accounting* – The activities concerned with identifying the actual costs of delivering IT services, comparing these with budgeted costs, and managing variance from the budget. It builds on good administration of costs and expenditures, and requires specific accountancy skills.
- *Charging* – The activities concerned with payment for IT services. Charging for IT services is optional, and many organizations choose to treat their internal IT service provider as a cost centre. Charging includes billing.

Budgeting is the activity of predicting and controlling the spending of money, based on cost projections and workload forecasting.

Budgeting consists of a periodic negotiation cycle to set future budgets (usually annual) and the routine monitoring and adjusting of current budgets. This is executed by all managers who have responsibility for any level of expenditure or income. Since each manager understands their part of the organization best, they will define their plans, and the budgets that will enable them to execute those plans.

Accounting can be supported by *cost models*: frameworks that allow the service provider to determine and allocate the costs of providing services. Cost models enable the understanding of how costs are spent, and how changes and trends impact the costs of services:

- *Cost by IT organization* – When the service provider has multiple IT organizations, each of these units can account for their own cost and report these to a central unit where the costs are allocated to the various business units.
- *Cost by service* – Often used by professional external service providers that operate in an open market. Customers can be informed about the cost or price of a specific service.
- *Cost by customer* – Rarely used on its own, since it involves communicating the actual costs of components within the service provider to the customer. Often used effectively for providing desktop equipment and support, and software licensing for personal productivity software.
- *Cost by location* – Also rarely used on its own, since it involves communicating the actual costs of components within the service provider to a group of customers at a particular location.

Most cost models are actually *hybrid cost models* that employ a number of different types of cost model for various purposes and situations.

Costs that are not easily related to services, overheads such as the cost of the CIO (chief information officer) and general IT management, should also be allocated. The enterprise financial management policies will define policies for how to deal with these *unallocated costs*.

A *cost centre* is anything to which a cost can be allocated – for example, a service, location, department, business unit etc. That cost centre might become the basis for a charging policy or billing method. Cost centres are used to determine which costs are direct and which are indirect. They also provide meaningful categories for allocating and reporting costs so that they can be understood and influenced by a wide audience.

A *cost unit* is the lowest level category to which costs will be allocated. Cost units are usually things that can be easily measured and communicated in terms to which customers can relate.

In accounting, the categories to record expenses should be meaningful for the type of services being provided and the resources that are used to deliver the services. Categories should reflect the practices, procedures and culture of the organization. Costs can be mainly defined as cost types and cost elements:

- *Cost types* – The highest level of category to which costs are assigned in budgeting and accounting, for example, hardware, software, people, consulting services and facilities.
- *Cost elements* – Sub categories of cost types, for example the cost type 'people' could have cost elements of payroll, staff benefits, expenses, training, overtime etc.

Costs can be classified as follows:
- *Capital or operational* – Capital costs or capital expenditure (Capex) is the cost of purchasing something that will become a financial asset – for example equipment and buildings. Operational costs or operational expenditure (Opex) is the cost resulting from running the IT services, which often involves repeating payments – for example, staff costs, hardware maintenance and electricity.
- *Direct or indirect* – Direct costs can be allocated in full to a specific customer, service, cost centre, project etc. (for example, the cost of providing dedicated servers or personal computers). Indirect costs cannot be allocated in full. They are sometimes known as overheads, and allocated using a separate 'uplift' calculation.
- *Fixed or variable* – Fixed costs are costs that do not vary with IT service usage – for example, the cost of server hardware. Variable costs are costs that depend on how much an IT service is used, how many products are produced, the number and type of users, electricity or something else that cannot be fixed in advance.

Methods for allocating indirect costs include:
- *Activity-based costing* – An accurate, but expensive and complex, method where all involved activities are determined, measured, calculated, and allocated to a cost centre.
- *Utilization-based allocation* – Costs are allocated based on the relative use by a cost centre.
- *Agreed basis for allocation* – If there is no straightforward method for allocation, the service provider can still agree with the business how costs will be allocated. This requires easy to measure methods that are considered fair by the business.

This could be number of users, number of PCs or something else.

- *Indirect cost rate* – Regardless of what method of allocation is used, there are always costs that cannot be easily allocated. The indirect cost rate method sets a consistent rate to allocate these costs.

Fixed assets do not retain their value for ever. The reduction in value of an asset over its life is called *depreciation.* The reduction in value is based on wearing out, consumption, or other reduction in the useful economic value.

Accounting should have *action plans* in place to cope with significant deviation from agreed financial targets. These action plans are normally short term, and are aimed at restoring the organization to its planned path within a month or quarter, or else getting the stakeholders to agree to change the original plans and targets. Reporting budget deviation on its own achieves little but awareness. A budget deviation with an associated action plan is a powerful management tool.

Charging is the activity whereby payment is required for services delivered. For internal service providers charging is optional. If internal IT service providers are used as a cost centre, they usually do not charge their customers. Cost recovery is then done through a 'chargeback' system that uses the central financial function. External service providers always charge for their services, as part of their business.

Charging can be beneficial, since it places the customer in control of their IT spend, and it provides the business with more accurate information. Charging stimulates *cost awareness*, and can encourage better, or different, use of IT services to support business outcomes at optimal cost. Charging can also be complex and bureaucratic, using expensive tools. Charging has to be simple, fair and realistic to be successful.

If charging is chosen as a means for recovering costs, the level of cost recovery needs to be defined:

- *Cost recovery or break-even* – IT will only seek to recover its costs and not make a profit or loss.
- *Recovery with an additional margin* – IT will seek to recover more than its actual costs. An internal IT service provider should carefully motivate the margin, for example as a financial reservation for innovation and renewal.
- *Cross-subsidization* – A subset of services may be charged with an additional margin, which is then applied to offset the cost of another subset of services.
- *Notional charging* – This is actually only financial reporting, raising cost awareness. Notional charging is a way of telling an internal customer how much a service would cost them if they were paying for it directly.

Whenever charging is implemented, it should include a conscious policy to monitor the impact of charging on behaviour and tune the charging system to deal with each situation.

Pricing is the activity for establishing how much customers will be charged. Pricing strategies can be chosen to influence customer behavior, and include:

- *Cost* – This option is based on a break-even or cost recovery model. The chargeable item is priced as close as possible to the actual cost of the cost units.
- *Cost plus* – The basic form is: Price = cost + x% mark-up.

- *Going rate* – The price is comparable with the price used by similar service providers in similar organizations.
- *Market price* – The price is the same as that charged by external suppliers.
- *Fixed price* – The IT organization sets a price based upon negotiation with the customer, which covers a set period and a predicted consumption.
- *Tiered subscription* – Here a service is being priced differently according to the service package option that has been selected.
- *Differential charging* – Setting different charges for different usage of the same or similar services enables an organization to reward some usage patterns over others.

When charging is implemented, the final step in the process would be billing. *Billing* involves producing and presenting an invoice for services to a customer. There are three main options for billing:

- *No billing* – Internal service providers do not have to produce an invoice of any type, as long as costs can be allocated to other business units. External service providers are required to submit invoices in order to receive payment.
- *Informational billing (notional charging)* – This can be used by internal service providers, as part of a notional charging policy. The service provider produces an invoice but does not actually go through the process of collecting revenue.
- *Billing and collection (real charging)* – This is used by an external service provider. It can also be used by an internal service provider if it involves internal transfer (internal customer), but requires highly detailed financial systems.

3.7 Demand management

Introduction

Demand management is a vital aspect of service management. It aligns supply with demand and seeks to understand, anticipate and influence customer demand for services and the provision of capacity to meet these demands.

Service management must deal with the additional problem of synchronous production and consumption. Service operation is impossible without the existence of a demand that consumes the product. It is a pull-system, in which consumption cycles stimulate the production cycles (Figure 3.2).

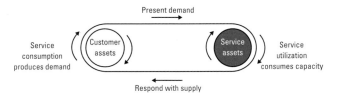

Figure 3.2 Close relationship between demand and capacity
Source: the Cabinet Office

It is not possible to produce service output and store it until demand arises. The production capacity of the resources available for a service is therefore adjusted in accordance with demand prognoses and patterns.

It is extremely important to study the customer's business and thus identify, analyze and record patterns. This creates a sufficient basis for capacity management.

Basic concepts

Demand management is all about matching demand and supply, in a proactive way. It looks at the expected future behavior of customers and the capacity of the service provider and tries to match these in an optimal way. This requires a good understanding of patterns of business activity (PBAs) of the customer. Demand management is active throughout the service lifecycle.

Demand management identifies and analyses patterns of business activities (PBAs) to understand the levels of demand that will be placed on a service. *Activity-based demand management*: business processes are the primary source of demand for services. PBAs have an impact on demand patterns.

Demand management also defines and analyses user profiles (UPs) to understand the typical profiles of demand for services from different types of user.

Demand management is typically a proactive process that works closely with capacity management to ensure that business demand is balanced with the provider's capacity, at the lowest cost possible.

A *service package* is a collection of two or more services that have been combined to offer a solution to a specific type of customer need or to underpin specific business outcomes. A service package can consist of a combination of core services, enabling services and enhancing services.

Core services deliver the basic results to the customer. They represent the value that customers require and for which they are willing to pay. Core services represent the basis for the value-proposition to the customer. Additional services that may or may not be visible to customers enable that value proposition (*enabling services* or basic factors) or improve it (*enhancing services* or excitement factors).

Activities

Bundling core services and enabling and enhancing services is a vital aspect of a market strategy. Service providers should thoroughly analyze the prevailing conditions in their business environment, the needs of the customer segments or types they serve, and the alternatives that are available to these customers. These are strategic decisions – they shape a long-term vision that is intended to enable the organization to create lasting value for customers, even if the methods, standards, technologies and regulations in an industry change. Bundling supporting services with core services affects service operation and represents challenges for the design, transition and CSI (continual service improvement) stages.

Service providers must focus on the effective delivery of value through core services, while at the same time keeping an eye on the supporting services. Research has shown that customers are often dissatisfied with supporting services. Some supporting services, such as the helpdesk or technical support, are generally bundled but can also be offered separately. This is an important consideration in the strategic planning and review of the plans. These strategic decisions can have a major impact on the service provider's success at the portfolio level. They are important primarily to service providers who supply multiple organizations or business units (BU's) while at the same time being forced to reduce costs in order to preserve the competitiveness of their portfolio.

Business processes are the primary inputs for demand management. Patterns of business activity (PBAs) influence the demand forecasts and patterns. Analyzing PBAs within demand management can deliver inputs to other service management processes such as:

- *Service design* – To make the design suit the demand patterns.
- *Service catalogue management* – To have the appropriate services available.
- *Service portfolio management* – To approve investing in additional capacity, new services, changes to services.
- *Financial management for IT services* – To approve suitable incentives to influence demand.

3.8   Business relationship management

Introduction

Business relationship management is the process that manages the links between the service provider and customers at the strategic and tactical levels to ensure that the service provider understands the business requirements of the customer and is able to provide services that meet these needs.

Basic concepts

Business relationship management aims at establishing and maintaining a business relationship between the service provider and the customer. For that purpose the service provider should understand the customer and its business needs.

Business relationship management identifies the continually changing customer needs and ensures that the service provider is able to meet these. Business relationship management also manages the customer's expectations.

The primary measure of whether the purpose of business relationship management is being achieved is the level of customer satisfaction.

Activities

The business relationship manager (BRM) ensures that the service provider understands the customer's perspective of service and is able to prioritize its services and service assets appropriately. Core to the process is managing the relationship with the customer. For that purpose the provider needs to understand the customer's business and should be aware of any relevant changes to the customer's business.

The process is not only reactive; it also monitors trends in the technology environment to spot opportunities for the customer's business.

In the process of aligning the services to the customer's needs, the business relationship management process supports the determination of business requirements for new or changing services.

Managing the relationship also includes mediation in conflicts, and the regular management of customer complaints, opportunities, requests, and compliments.

The business relationship management process is either triggered by the customer, or by the service management processes. This can relate to anything influencing the customer relationship, and includes customer requirements, requests, complaints, escalations or compliments. The process uses the service strategy and the service portfolio, as well as the SLAs.

3.9   Governance

Governance is what defines the common directions, policies and rules that both the business and IT use to conduct business. It is usually expressed in a set of strategies, policies and plans. These are created with three main activities:

- *Evaluate* – The ongoing evaluation of the organization's performance and its environment.
- *Direct* – Communicating the strategy, policies and plans to, and through, management, ensuring that all management staff has appropriate guidelines available to comply with governance.
- *Monitor* – Here, the deliverables of the organization are reviewed against the initial directives, to determine compliance with governance settings. Measures are taken if necessary.

Governance differs essentially from management. Governance is performed by governors who evaluate, direct and control the organization in terms of the set strategy, policies and plans. Management is performed by executives and their staff, who execute the activities of the organization according to the strategy, policies and plans: they realize the goals of the organization.

Governance can be supported by a framework like ISO/IEC 38500, containing a structured set of guidelines and documents that clearly articulate the strategy, policies and plans of the organization. Management can be supported by a service management system (SMS), to direct and control the service management activities.

3.10 Organization

There are five recognizable stages in organizational development within the spectrum of centralization and decentralization:

- *Stage 1: Network* – An organization in stage 1 focuses on fast, informal and ad hoc provision of services. The organization is technologically oriented and is uncomfortable with formal structures.
- *Stage 2: Directive* – In stage 2, the informal structure of stage 1 is transformed into an hierarchical structure with a strong management team. They assume the responsibility for leading the strategy and for guiding managers to embrace their functional responsibilities.
- *Stage 3: Delegation* – In stage 3, efforts are made to enhance technical efficiency and provide space for innovation in order to reduce costs and improve services.
- *Stage 4: Coordination* – In stage 4 the focus is directed towards the use of formal systems as a means of achieving better coordination.
- *Stage 5: Collaboration* – During stage 5, the focus is on the improvement of cooperation with the business.

The goal of the service strategy stage is to improve the core competencies. Sometimes it is more efficient to outsource certain services. We call this the SoC principle (separation of concerns, SoC): that which results from the search for competitive differentiation through the redistribution of resources and capabilities.

The following generic forms of outsourcing can be delineated:

- *Internal outsourcing*:
  - *Type 1 Internal* – Provision and delivery of services by internal staff; this offers the most control, but is limited in scale.

- *Type 2 Shared services* – Working with internal BUs; offers lower costs than Type 1 and more standardization, but is still limited in scale.
- *Traditional outsourcing*:
  - *Complete outsourcing of a service* – A single contract with one service provider; better in terms of scaling opportunities, but limited in best-in-class capabilities.
- *Multi-vendor outsourcing*:
  - *Prime* – A single contract with one service provider who works with multiple providers; improved capabilities and risks, but increased complexity.
  - *Consortium* – A selection of multiple service providers; the advantage is best-in class with more oversight; the disadvantage is the risk of the necessity of working with the competition.
  - *Selective outsourcing* – A pool of service providers selected and managed through the service receiver; this is the most difficult structure to manage.
  - *Co-Sourcing* – A variation of selective outsourcing in which the service receiver combines a structure of internal or shared services with external providers; in this case, the service receiver is the service integrator.

3.11 Methods, techniques and tools

Services are socio-technical systems with service assets as the operational elements. The effectiveness of service strategy depends on a well-managed relationship between the social and technical sub-systems. It is essential to identify and manage these dependencies and influences.

Tools for the service strategy stage can be:
- *Simulation* – System Dynamics is a methodology for understanding and managing the complex problems of IT organizations.
- *Analytical modeling* – Six Sigma, PMBOK® and PRINCE2® offer well tested methods based on analytical models. They must be evaluated and adopted within the context of service strategy and service management.

Three techniques for quantifying the value of an investment are suggested:
- *Business case* – A way of identifying business objectives that are dependent on service management.
- *Pre-Program ROI* – Techniques used to quantitatively analyze investments before committing resources.
- *Post-Program ROI* – Techniques used to retroactively analyze investments.

3.12 Implementation and operation

Strategic goals are to be converted into plans with objectives and ultimate goals, based on the lifecycle. Plans translate the intentions of the strategy into actions, through service design, service transition, service operation, and continual service improvement.

Service strategy provides every stage of the lifecycle with input:
- *Strategy and design* – Service strategies are implemented through the delivery of the portfolio in a specific market area. Newly chartered services or services that require improvements in order to suit the demand are promoted to the service design stage. The design can be driven by service models, outcomes, constraints or pricing.

- *Strategy and transition* – To reduce the risk of failing, all strategic changes go through service transition. Service transition processes analyze, evaluate and approve strategic initiatives. Service strategy provides service transition with structures and constraints like the service portfolio, policies, architectures, and the contract portfolio.
- *Strategy and operations* – The final realization of strategy occurs in the production stage. The strategy must be in line with operational capabilities and constraints. Deployment patterns in service operation define operational strategies for customers. Service operation is responsible for delivering the contract portfolio and should be able to deal with demand changes.
- *Strategy and CSI* – Due to constant changes, strategies are never static. Service strategies need to be developed, adopted and continually reviewed. Strategic imperatives influence quality perspectives processed in CSI. CSI processes deliver feedback for the strategy stage on, for example: quality perspective, warranty factors, reliability, maintainability, redundancy.

Challenges and opportunities:
- *Complexity* – IT organizations are complex systems. This explains why some service organizations are not inclined to change. Organizations are not always in a position to anticipate the long-term consequences of decisions and actions. Without continual learning processes, today's decisions often end up as tomorrow's problems.
- *Coordination and control* – The people who make the decisions often have limited time, attention and capacity. Therefore they delegate the roles and responsibilities to

teams and individuals. This makes coordination through cooperation and monitoring essential.

- *Preserving Value* – Customers are not only interested in the utility and warranty that they receive for the price they pay. They want to know the total cost of utilization (TCU).
- *Effectiveness in measurement* – Measurements focus the organization on its strategic goals, follow the progression and provide the organization with feedback. Most IT organizations are good at monitoring data, but often they are not very good at providing insights into the effectiveness of the services that they offer. It is crucial to perform the right analyses and to modify them as the strategy changes.

The implementation of strategy leads to changes in the service portfolio. This involves management of related risks. Risk is defined as follows: "a risk is an uncertain outcome, or in other words, a positive opportunity or a negative threat." Risk assessment and risk management must be applied to the service catalogue and service catalogue in order to identify, curb and mitigate the risks within the lifecycle stages.

The following types of risks are recognized:
- contract risks
- design risks
- operational risks
- market risks.

There are four main types of service management implementation strategies:
- *Even keel mode* – The organization sees no problem with IT service management, does not need growth, and is rather content with the current situation.

- *Trouble mode* – The organization understands that significant action is required, since there are a significant number of problems. A more comprehensive management approach is needed.
- *Growth mode* – The organization is well aware of significant improvements being required. It understands the contribution of IT to strategic business goals, and works on a comprehensive, strategic approach to improve IT service management.
- *Radical change mode* – The organization is going through a fundamental change as an organization (outsourcing, merger, acquisition) and required a quick improvement of their IT service management.

Which of these basic patterns is suited best to a specific organization depends on the current state of the organization.

4 Lifecycle stage: service design

4.1 Introduction
Service design deals with the design and development of services and their related processes. The most important objective of service design is: the design of new or changed services for introduction into a test or production environment.

The service design stage in the lifecycle begins with the demand for new or changed requirements from the customer. Good preparation and an effective and efficient infusion of people, processes, products (services, technology and tools) and partners (suppliers, manufacturers and vendors) – ITIL's four Ps – are a must if the design, plans and projects are to succeed.

4.2 Basic concepts
The design stage should cover five important aspects:
1. *The design of service solutions* – A structured design approach is necessary in order to produce a new service against appropriate costs, functionality, quality and compliant to agreed requirements, resources and capabilities. The process must be iterative and incremental in order to meet the customers' changing wishes and requirements. It is important to assemble a service design package (SDP) with all aspects of the (new or changed) service and its requirements through each stage of its lifecycle.
2. *The design of management information systems and tools, especially the service portfolio* – These instruments should be reviewed to make sure they can support the new or changed service. The service portfolio is a critical management system

for supporting all of the processes. It describes the service delivery in terms of value for the customer and must include all of the service information and its status. The portfolio illustrates the status of a service, whether in development, in production or retired.

3. *The design of the architecture* – The activities include preparing the blueprints for the development and deployment of an IT infrastructure, the applications, the data and the environment (according to the needs of the business). Architectures to be reviewed should include technology architectures as well as management architectures.

4. *The design of processes* – By defining what the activities in the lifecycle stages are and what the inputs and outputs are, it is possible to work more efficiently and effectively, and in a more customer-oriented way. By assessing the current quality of processes and the options for improvement, the organization can enhance its efficiency and effectiveness even further. This does not only relate to processes in the design stage, but to processes in all stages, as well as to roles, responsibilities and skills. All of these should be in place to support and maintain the new or changed service.

5. *The design of measurement methods and metrics* – In order to lead and manage the development process of services effectively, regular assessments of service quality must be performed, and relevant metrics must be available. The selected assessment system must be synchronized with the capacity and maturity of the processes that are assessed. There are four elements that can be investigated: *progress, compliance, effectiveness* and *efficiency of the process*.

The question which model should be used for the development of IT services largely depends on the *service delivery model* that is chosen. The delivery options are:

- *Insourcing* – Internal resources are used for the design, development, maintenance, execution, and/or support for the service.
- *Outsourcing* – Engaging an external organization for the design, development, maintenance, execution, and/or support of the service.
- *Co-sourcing* – A combination of Insourcing and outsourcing in which various outsourcing organizations work cooperatively throughout the service lifecycle.
- *Multi-sourcing* – (or partnership) Multiple organizations make formal agreements with the focus on strategic partnerships (creating new market opportunities).
- *Business process outsourcing (BPO)* – An external organization provides and manages (part of) another organization's business processes in another location.
- *Application service provision* – Computer-based services are offered to the customer over a network.
- *Knowledge process outsourcing (KPO)* – Provides domain-based processes and business expertise

Traditional *development approaches* are based on the principle that the requirements of the customer can be determined at the beginning of the service lifecycle and that the development costs can be kept under control by managing the changes. Rapid application development (RAD) approaches begin with the notion that change is inevitable and that discouraging change simply indicates passivity in regard to the market. The RAD-approach is an incremental and iterative development approach:

- *The incremental approach* – A service is designed bit by bit. Parts are developed separately and are delivered individually. Each piece supports one of the business functions that the entire service needs. The big advantage in this approach is its

shorter delivery time. The development of each part, however, requires that all stages of the lifecycle are traversal.
- *The iterative approach* – The development lifecycle is repeated several times. Techniques like prototyping are used in order to understand the customer-specific requirements better.

A combination of the two approaches is possible. An organization can begin by specifying the requirements for the entire service, followed by an incremental design and the development of the software. Many organizations however, choose standard software solutions to satisfy needs and demands instead of designing the service themselves.

4.3 Processes and other activities
This section explains the processes and activities of the service design.

Service design processes:
- *Design coordination* – The design coordination process supports the entire design stage by providing a single comprehensive coordination process for all activities in the service design stage.
- *Service catalogue management (SCM)* – The goal of SCM is the development and maintenance of a service catalogue that includes accurate details of all services, whether operational, in development or retired, and the business processes they support.
- *Service level management(SLM)* – The goal of SLM is to ensure that the levels of IT service delivery are documented, agreed and achieved, for both existing services and future services in accordance with the agreed targets.

- *Capacity management* – The goal of capacity management is to ensure that the capacity corresponds to both the existing and future needs of the customer (recorded in a capacity plan).
- *Availability management* – The goal of the availability management process is to ensure that the availability level of both new and changed services corresponds with the levels as agreed with the customer. It must maintain an availability management information system (AMIS) which forms the basis the availability plan.
- *IT service continuity management (ITSCM)* – The ultimate goal of ITSCM is to support business continuity (vital business functions, VBF) by ensuring that the required IT facilities can be restored within the agreed time.
- *Information security management* – The goal of information security management is to ensure that the information security policy meets the organization's overall security policy and the requirements originating from corporate governance.
- *Supplier management* – The goal of supplier management is to manage all suppliers and contracts in order to support the delivery of services to the customer.

Service design technology-related activities:
- *Requirements engineering* – Understanding and documenting the business and user's requirements (functional requirements, management and operational requirements and usability requirements).
- *Management of data and information* – Data is one of the most critical matters that must be kept under control in order to develop, deliver and support effective IT services.

- *Management of applications* – Applications, along with data and infrastructure, comprise the technical components of IT services.

4.4 Design coordination

Introduction
The design coordination process supports the entire design stage by providing a single comprehensive coordination process for all activities in the service design stage. The main value of the design coordination process to the business is the production of a set of consistent designs that will provide the desired business outcomes.

Basic concepts
The design coordination process is basically a process that oversees the other processes in the service design stage of the lifecycle. It monitors the correct use of documents, policies, and standard in each of the processes, and the timely execution of activities, In cases of conflicts between processes, it manages the escalation of issues.

Activities
The process includes the support of projects and changes, the maintenance of all relevant guidelines, resource management, performance management of all design activities, ensuring that all requirements are appropriately addressed, and managing the handover of required products to the service transition stage.

Overall lifecycle stage activities include:
- *Define and maintain policies and methods* – The design coordination process should ensure that throughout this

lifecycle stage a common set of agreed policies, architectures, methods and principles is used to support consistent, reliable and repeatable design processes.

- *Plan design resources and capabilities* – The resources and capabilities required for new or changed services need to be available for each of the design processes. This includes hiring and training staff, and making new technologies available for design processes.
- *Coordinate design activities* – All design activities need to be coordinated across projects and changes. Schedules, resources, escalations, suppliers, and support teams must be managed throughout the design lifecycle stage.
- *Manage design risks and issues* – Risks should be assessed and managed, to ensure quality and continual improvement.
- *Improve service design* – Continual improvement activities are based on monitoring the performance of service design activities.

Individual design activities include:
- *Plan individual designs* – For each project or change, the design activities need to be planned carefully to ensure that the design can deliver the required business outcomes.
- *Coordinate individual designs* – Individual changes and projects require the operational coordination of design activities, to ensure that all activities are executed according to agreed plans and policies.
- *Monitor individual designs* – Being responsible for the overall delivery, the design coordination process should monitor individual progress of designs.
- *Review designs and ensure handover of SDPs* – At the end of the stage all deliverables, including the SDPs, should be formally reviewed against agreed plans.

4.5 Service catalogue management

Introduction

The purpose of service catalogue management (SCM) is the development and upkeep of a service catalogue that contains all details, status, possible interactions and mutual dependencies of all present services and those under development. The service catalogue includes information about deliverables, prices, contact points, ordering and request processes.

Basic concepts

Over years, an organization's IT infrastructure grows at a steady pace. For this reason, it is difficult to obtain an accurate picture of the services offered by the organization and to whom they are offered. To get a clearer picture, a service portfolio is developed (with a service catalogue as part of it), and kept up-to-date. The development of the service portfolio is a component of the service strategy stage.

It is important to make a clear distinction between the service portfolio and the service catalogue:
- *Service portfolio* – The service portfolio contains information about each service and its status. As a result, the portfolio describes the entire process, starting with the client requirements for the development, building and execution of the service. The service portfolio represents all active and inactive services in the various stages of the lifecycle.
- *Service catalogue* – The service catalogue is a subset of the service portfolio and only consists of active and approved services (at user level) in service operation. The service catalogue divides services into components. It contains

policies, guidelines and responsibilities, as well as prices, service level agreements and delivery conditions.

Many organizations integrate and maintain the service portfolio and service catalogue as a part of their configuration management system (CMS). By defining every service the organization can relate the incidents and requests for change to the services in question. Therefore changes in both service portfolio and service catalogue must be included in the change management process.

The service catalogue can also be used for a business impact analysis (BIA) as part of IT service continuity management (ITSCM), or as a starting point for the re-distribution of the workload as part of capacity management. These benefits justify the investment (in time and money) involved in preparing a catalogue and making it worthwhile.

The service catalogue should provide clear and relevant information to its users. Because these users can be different, it is advised to create different views of the service catalogue. Views of a two-view service catalogue can relate to the following services:

- *Customer-facing services* – These are IT services that are visible to the customer. They normally support the customer's business processes and facilitate desired outcomes.
- *Supporting services* – These are IT services that support or 'underpin' the customer-facing services. The customer normally doesn't actually 'see' these services, although they are essential to the delivery of customer-facing IT services.

A three-view service catalogue could be created by splitting the customer-facing services up in two: a wholesale customer view and a retail customer view. Views must be tailor made for each company.

A combination of both aspects provides a quick overview on the impact of incidents and changes. For this reason, many mature organizations combine both aspects in a service catalogue, as part of a service portfolio.

Activities
The service catalogue is the only resource which contains constant information about all services of the service provider. The catalogue should be accessible to every authorized person. Activities include:
- defining the services
- producing and maintaining an accurate service catalogue
- providing information about the service catalogue to stakeholders
- interfacing with all stakeholders (business, support teams, suppliers, SLM, business relationship management, and internal teams) to ensure the accuracy of the service catalogue and the alignment with stakeholder interests.

4.6 Service level management

Introduction
The objective of the service level management (SLM) process is to agree on the delivery of IT services and to make sure that the agreed level of IT service provision is attained.

Basic concepts

The SLM process entails planning, coordinating, supplying, agreeing, monitoring and reporting on *service level agreements* (SLAs). This also includes the ongoing review of the service. This ensures that the quality of the service satisfies the agreed requirements and can be improved where possible. The SLA is a written agreement between a service provider and a customer containing mutual goals and responsibilities. Options for SLAs are:

- *service-based SLAs* – the SLA covers one service for all customers of that service
- *customer-based SLAs* – the SLA covers all services used by a specific customer group
- *multi-level SLAs* – there is a structure of SLAs covering separate domains, e.g. a structure of corporate level SLAs, customer level SLAs and service level SLAs.

An *operational level agreement* (OLA) is an agreement between an IT service provider and another part of the same organization. An OLA defines the goods or services to be provided from one department to the other, and the responsibilities of both parties.

An *underpinning contract (UC)* is a contract with a third party, in support of the delivery of an agreed IT service to a customer. The UC defines targets and responsibilities that are required to meet agreed service level targets in an SLA.

There is a close relationship between service level management and business relationship management. Both processes aim to understand the customer's needs and ensure customer satisfaction. Complaints and compliments are logged and managed in close cooperation. Both use customer satisfaction surveys, and use these to improve the alignment between provider and customer. The focus of these processes may differ: business relationship management is more involved with overall customer satisfaction, and SLM is more focused on achieving agreed individual service levels.

For reporting service achievements against service targets, the provider may use an SLA monitoring (SLAM) chart. A simple SLAM chart may provide an overview of the performance expressed in the colors red, amber, and green (also known as a RAG chart).

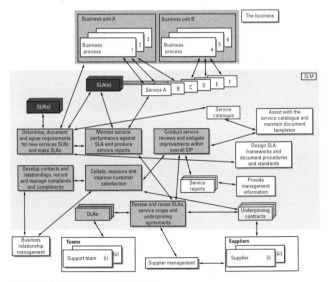

Figure 4.1 Service level management
Source: the Cabinet Office

Activities

The activities of service level management (Figure 4.1) are:

- *Designing SLM frameworks* – SLM has to design the best possible SLA, so that all services can be provided and clients can be serviced in a manner that meets mutual needs.
- *Determining, documenting and agreeing on the requirements for new services and producing service level requirements (SLRs)* – When the service catalogue is made and the SLA structure determined, the first SLR (a customer requirement for an aspect of a service) needs to be determined.
- *Monitoring the performance with regard to the SLA and reporting the outcome* – Everything incorporated into the SLA must be measurable. Otherwise, disputes may arise, which may result in damaged confidence.
- *Improving client satisfaction* – Besides the "hard" criteria it should also be noted how the customer experiences the service rendered, in terms of "soft" criteria.
- *Reviewing the underlying agreements* – The IT service provider is also dependent on its own internal technical services and external partners; in order to satisfy the SLA targets, the underlying agreements with internal departments (OLAs) and external suppliers (UCs) must support the SLA.
- *Reviewing and improving services* – Regularly consult the customer to evaluate the services and make possible improvements in the service provision; focus on those improvement items that yield the greatest benefit to the business. Improvement activities should be based on this service review and documented and managed in a service improvement plan (SIP).
- *Developing contacts and relationships* – SLM has to instill confidence in the business. With the service catalogue, SLM can start working proactively; the catalogue supplies

information that improves the understanding of the relation between services, business units and processes.

4.7 Availability management

Introduction
Availability management has to ensure that the delivered availability levels for all services comply with or exceed the agreed requirements in a cost-effective manner.

Basic concepts
Figure 4.2 illustrates a number of starting points for availability management. The unavailability of services can be reduced by aiming to reduce each of the stages distinguished in the *extended incident lifecycle*.

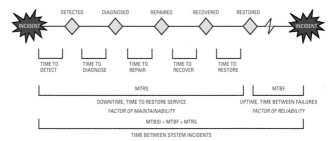

Figure 4.2 The extended incident lifecycle

Services must be restored quickly when they are unavailable to users. The *mean time to restore service (MTRS)* is the time within which a function (service, system or component) is back up after a failure. The MTRS depends on a number of factors, such as:
- configuration of service assets
- MTRS of individual components

- competencies of support personnel
- available resources
- policy plans
- procedures
- redundancy.

Other metrics for measuring availability include:
- *Mean time between failures (MTBF)* – The average time that a CI or service can perform its agreed function without interruption.
- *Mean time between service incidents (MTBSI)* – The mean time from when a system or service fails, until it next fails.
- *Mean time to repair (MTTR)* – The average time taken to repair a CI or service after a failure. MTTR is measured from when the CI or service fails until it is repaired. MTTR does not include the time required to recover or restore.

Availability management operates at two inter-connected levels:
- *Component availability* – This involves all aspects of component availability and unavailability.
- *Service availability* – This involves all aspects of service availability and unavailability and the impact of component availability, or the potential impact of component unavailability on service availability. Service availability measures end-to-end service.

The *reliability* of a service or component indicates how long it can perform its agreed function without interruption.

The *maintainability* of a service or component indicates how fast it can be restored after a failure.

The *serviceability* describes the ability of a third party supplier to meet the terms of their contract, which includes agreed levels of reliability, maintainability or availability for a CI.

The reliability of systems can be increased through various types of *redundancy*.

Due to increased dependency upon IT services, customers often require services with *high availability*. This requires a design that considers the elimination of single points of failure (SPOFs) and/or the provision of alternative components to provide minimal disruption to the business operation should an IT component failure occur.

High Availability solutions make use of techniques such as Fault Tolerance, resilience and fast recovery to reduce the number of incidents, and the impact of incidents.

Activities

Availability management must continually ensure that all services comply with the objectives. New or changed services must be designed in such a way that they comply with the objectives. To realize this, availability management can perform reactive and proactive activities (Figure 4.3):

- *Reactive activities* – Executed in the operational stage of the lifecycle:
  - monitoring, measuring, analyzing and reporting the availability of services and components
  - unavailability analysis
  - expanded lifecycle of the incident
  - service failure analysis (SFA)
- *Proactive activities* – Executed in the design stage of the lifecycle:

- identifying vital business functions (VBFs), the part of a business process that is critical to the success of the business
- designing for availability
- component failure impact analysis (CFIA)
- single point of failure (SPOF) analysis
- fault tree analysis (FTA)
- modeling to test and analyze predicted availabilities
- risk assessment and management
- availability test schemes
- planned and preventive maintenance
- production of the projected service outage (PSO) document (identifying the effect of planned changes, maintenance activities and test plans on agreed service levels)
- continual reviewing and improvement.

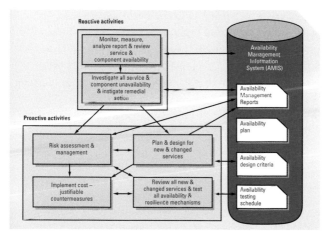

Figure 4.3 Availability management
Source: the Cabinet Office

4.8 Capacity management

Introduction
Capacity management has to provide IT capacity coinciding with both the current and future needs of the customers balanced against justifiable costs. Service strategy analyzes the wishes and requirements of customers; in the service design stage, capacity management is a critical success factor for defining an IT service.

Basic concepts
The *capacity management information system (CMIS)* provides relevant information on the capacity and performance of services in order to support the capacity management process. This information system is one of the most important elements in the capacity management process.

The CMIS information is used by the service provider in a *capacity plan*, to administer the current usage of service and components, and to plan the capacity of the IT infrastructure, in order to meet the growing or declining needs of existing and new services. The capacity plan should be actively used as a basis for decision-making.

Activities
The capacity management process consists of:
- *reactive activities*:
  - monitoring and measuring
  - responding and reacting to capacity related events
- *proactive activities*:
  - predicting future requirements and trends
  - budgeting, planning and implementing upgrades
  - seeking ways to improve service performance
  - optimizing the performance of a service.

Some activities (Figure 4.4) must be executed repeatedly (proactively or reactively). They provide basic information and triggers for other activities and processes in capacity management. For instance:
- monitoring IT usage and response times
- analyzing data
- tuning and implementation.

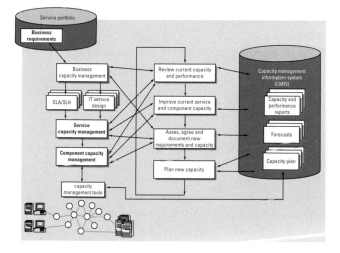

Figure 4.4 Capacity management overview with sub-processes
Source: the Cabinet Office

Capacity management can be an extremely technical, complex and demanding process that comprises three sub-processes:
- *Business capacity management* - Translates the customer's requirements into specifications for the service and IT infrastructure; focus on current and future requirements.

- *Service capacity management* – Identifies and understands the IT services (including the sources, patterns, etc) to make them comply with the defined targets.
- *Component capacity management (CCM)* – Manages, controls and predicts the performance, use and capacity of individual IT components.

All of the capacity management sub-processes analyze the information stored in the CMIS.

4.9 IT service continuity management

Introduction
IT service continuity management (ITSCM) has to support business continuity by ensuring that the required IT facilities (computer systems, networks, etc) can be resumed within the agreed timeframe. ITSCM manages the risks that could seriously affect IT services.

Basic concepts
Once service continuity or recovery plans have been created they need to be (kept) aligned with the *business continuity plans (BCPs)* and business priorities. Figure 4.5 shows the cyclic process of ITSCM and the role of overall *business continuity management (BCM)*.

Activities
The process consists of four stages:
- *Stage 1: Initiation* – This stage covers the entire organization and includes the following activities:
  - defining the policy
  - specifying the conditions and scope

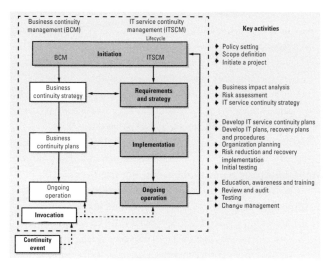

Figure 4.5 Lifecycle of IT service continuity management
Source: the Cabinet Office

- allocating resources (people, resources and funds)
- defining the project organization and management structure
- approving project and quality plans
- *Stage 2: Requirements and strategy* – Determining the business requirements for ITSCM is vital when investigating how well an organization can survive a calamity. This stage includes requirements and strategy. The requirements involve the performance of a business impact analysis and risk estimate:
  - *Requirement 1: Business impact analysis (BIA)* – Quantify the impact caused by the loss of services. If the impact can be determined in detail, it is called "hard impact" – e.g. financial losses. "Soft impact" is less easily determined.

It represents, for instance, the impact on Public Relations, morale and health.

- *Requirement 2: Risk assessment* – There are various risk analyses and methods. Risk assessment is an assessment of risks that may occur. Risk management identifies the response and counter-measures that can be taken. A standard method like Management of Risk (M_o_R) can be used to investigate and manage the risks.
- *Strategy 1: Risk-reducing measures* – Measures to reduce risks must be implemented in combination with availability management since failure reduction has an impact on service availability. Measures may include: fault tolerant systems, good IT security controls, and offsite storage.
- *Strategy 2: ITSCM recovery options* – The continuity strategy must weigh the costs of risk-reducing measures against the recovery measures (manual work-arounds, reciprocal arrangements, gradual recovery, intermediate recovery, fast recovery and immediate recovery) to restore critical processes.

- *Stage 3: Implementation* – The ITSCM plans can be created once the strategy is approved. The organization structure (leadership and decision-making processes) changes in a disaster recovery process. Set this up around a senior manager in charge.
- *Stage 4: Ongoing operation* – This stage includes:
  - education, awareness and training of personnel
  - review and audit
  - testing
  - change management (ensures that all changes have been studied for their potential impact)
  - ultimate test (invocation).

4.10 Information security management

Introduction
Information security management needs to align IT security with business security and has to ensure that information security is managed effectively in all services and service management operations.

Basic concepts
The information security management process and framework include:
- information security policy
- Information security management system (ISMS)
- comprehensive security strategy (related to the business objectives and strategy)
- effective security structure and controls
- risk management
- monitoring processes
- communication strategy
- training strategy.

The *information security policy* needs to be considered within the overall corporate security framework and should be supported by top executive management, including a wide spectrum of security issues. It should cover policies for asset control, password settings, the use of email and internet, anti-virus mechanisms, access, document control, etc.

The ISMS represents the basis for cost-effective development of an information security program that supports the business objectives. Use the *four Ps* of People, Processes, Products (including technology) and Partners (including suppliers) to ensure a high security level where required.

The framework can be based on ISO 27001, the international standard for information security management. Figure 4.6 is based on various recommendations, including ISO 27001, and provides information about the five elements (control, plan, implement, evaluate, maintain) and their separate objectives.

Figure 4.6 Framework for managing IT security
Source: the Cabinet Office

Activities

Information security management should include the following activities:

- operation, maintenance and distribution of an information security policy
- communication, implementation and enforcement of security policies
- assessment of information
- implementing (and documenting) controls that support the information security policy and manage risks

- monitoring and management of breaches and incidents
- proactive improvement of the control systems.

The information security manager must understand that security is not just a step in the lifecycle and that it cannot be guaranteed by technology alone. Information security is a continuous process and an integrated part of all services and systems. Figure 4.7 describes controls that can be used in the process.

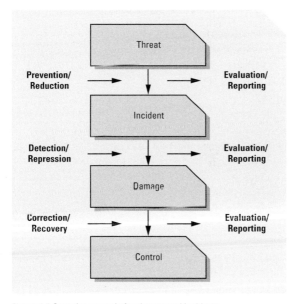

Figure 4.7 Security controls for threats and incidents
Source: the Cabinet Office

Figure 4.7 shows that a risk may result in a threat that in turn causes an incident, leading to damage. Various measures can be taken between these stages:

- *preventive measures* – prevent effects (e.g. access management)
- *reductive measures* – limit effects (e.g. backup and testing)
- *detective measures* – detect effects (e.g. monitoring)
- *repressive measures* – suppress effects (e.g. blocking)
- *corrective measures* – repair effects (e.g. rollback).

4.11 Supplier management

Introduction
Supplier management manages suppliers and the services they provide, it is aimed at securing consistent quality at the right price.

Basic concepts
All activities in this process must result from the supplier strategy and the service strategy policy. Create a supplier and contract management information system (SCMIS) to achieve consistency and effectiveness in implementing policy. Ideally, this database would be an integrated element of CMS or SKMS. The database should contain all details regarding suppliers and their contracts, together with details about the type of service or product, and any information and relationships to other configuration items.

The data stored here will provide important information for activities and procedures such as:
- categorizing of suppliers
- maintenance of supplier and contract database
- evaluation and building of new suppliers and contracts
- building new supplier relationships
- management of suppliers and contracts
- renewing and ending contracts.

Categorization of suppliers should support the appropriate level of effort spent on each supplier. Suppliers can be categorized as follows:

- *Strategic* – Significant 'partnering' relationships that involve sharing confidential strategic information to facilitate long-term plans. To be managed by senior management.
- *Tactical* – Relationships involving significant commercial activity and business interaction. To be managed by middle management.
- *Operational* – For suppliers of operational products or services. To be managed by junior operational management.
- *Commodity* – For suppliers providing low-value and/or readily available products and services, which could be alternatively sourced relatively easily.

Activities

For external suppliers, it is recommended that you draw up a formal contract with clearly defined, agreed upon and documented responsibilities and goals. You must manage this contract during its entire lifecycle (Figure 4.8).

These stages are:

1. *Definition of new supplier and contract requirements* – Produce a program of requirements (statement of requirement (SoR) and/or invitation to tender (ITT)), provide conformity of strategy and policy, and develop a business case.
2. *Evaluation of new suppliers and contracts* – Identify new business requirements and evaluate new suppliers as part of the service design process. They provide inputs for all other aspects of the lifecycle of the contract. Take various issues into account when selecting a new supplier, such as references, ability, and financial aspects.

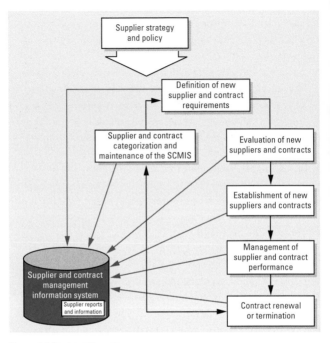

Figure 4.8 Contract lifecycle
Source: the Cabinet Office

3. *Supplier and contract categorization and maintenance of the SCMIS* – The amount of time and energy that should be put into a supplier depends on the impact of this supplier and its service. A subdivision could be made according to strategic relationships (managed by senior management), relationships at a tactical level (managed by middle management), execution level (execution management) and suppliers that only provide goods such as paper and cartridges. The SCMIS should be updated.

4. *Establishment of new suppliers and contracts* – Supplier services and contracts should now be set up, relationships should be established, followed by service transition.

5. *Supplier, contract, and performance management* – At an operational level, the integrated processes of the client organization and of the supplier must function efficiently. Questions should be:
   - Should the supplier conform to the organization's change management process?
   - How will the service desk inform the supplier if there are incidents?
   - How will CMS information be updated when CIs change?

   During the lifecycle of the contract, keep a close eye on the following two issues in order to minimize risks:
   - the performance of suppliers
   - the services, service scope and contract reviews in comparison with original business requirements

   Make sure that provisions are still in tune with what the business initially desired.

6. *Contract renewal or termination* – At a strategic level, see how the contract is functioning and how relevant it will be in the future, whether changes are necessary and what the commercial performance of the contract is. Benchmarking could be an appropriate instrument to compare the current service provision with that of other suppliers in the industry. If, as a result, the decision is made to end the relationship with the supplier, it is important to assess what the consequences will be in legal and financial areas, and how the client organization and service provision will be affected.

4.12 Service design technology-related activities

Service design also contains a number of typically technology-related activities: *requirements engineering, management of data and information*, and *management of applications*.

Requirements engineering

The requirements of the business, users and other stakeholders need to be understood and documented, so they can be tracked during their lifecycle.

There are three types of requirements for each system, namely:
- *Functional requirements* – describing the utility aspects of a service, focused on the business function.
- *Management – and operational requirements* – describing the warranty aspects of a service (also called non-functional requirements).
- *Usability requirements* – describing the ease-of-use for a user, including the look-and-feel.

To prevent problems in developing requirements, it is important to involve all stakeholders, including the customer, the users' community, and the service development team.

The *requirements document* is the core of this activity. This document contains each individual requirement in a standard template. Each requirement must be clear, unambiguous and reasonable, synchronized with the customer's objectives, and not in conflict with any of the other requirements. The instrument of SMART (specific, measureable, achievable/appropriate, realistic/relevant and timely/time-bound) can be used to support this.

The result can then be recorded in the *requirements catalogue*, the central repository of the requirements portfolio in the overall service portfolio, containing a register of all users' requirements. Requirements should also be prioritized (e.g. according to the MoSCoW approach: must have, should have, could have, won't have).

Management of data and information

Data is one of the most critical matters that must be kept under control in order to develop, deliver and support effective IT services. Data should be available to (only) authorized users, and the quality of data should be guaranteed to support business processes.

There are four management areas in the field of data and information management:

- *Management of data sources* – The sources should be clear and responsibilities must be assigned to the right person. This process is also known as data administration.
- *Management of data – and information technology* – This area relates to the management of IT and includes matters such as the design of databases and database management.
- *Management of information processes* – The data lifecycle (creating, collecting, accessing, modifying, storing, deleting and archiving of data) must be controlled. This often occurs in conjunction with application management.
- *Management of data standards and policy* – The organization must formulate standards and policy for data management as a component of the IT strategy.

Data can be classified on three levels:
- *Operational data* – This data is necessary for the continued functioning of the organization and is the least specific.
- *Tactical data* – This is data that is needed for line or higher management; among other things, this refers to historical data, distilled from management information systems.
- *Strategic data* – Refers to the long-term trends compared with external (market) information.

Responsibilities of the *data owner* include:
- determining who can create, revise, read and delete data
- consent given regarding the way in which data are stored for modification
- approves level of security
- agreeing business description and a purpose.

In defining IT services, it is important that management and operational data requirements be considered. Specifically in the following areas:
- restoration of lost data
- controlled access to data
- implementation of policy on archiving of data
- periodic monitoring of data integrity.

Management of applications

An application is defined by ITIL as: "Software that provides functions which are required by an IT service."

Each application may be part of more than one IT service.
An application runs on one or more servers or clients.

It is crucial that the applications that are provided correspond with the requirements of the customer. Two alternative approaches are necessary to implement application management, namely:

- *Service development lifecycle (SDLC)* – A systematic problem-solving approach for supporting the development of an IT service. Steps include feasibility study, analysis, design, testing, implementation, evaluation, and maintenance.
- *Application maintenance* – The other approach looks globally at all of the services in order to ensure a continuing process of managing and maintaining the applications. All applications are described consistently in the application portfolio, which is synchronized with the customers' requirements.

The *application framework* includes all management- and operational aspects and provides solutions for all of the management- and operational requirements for an application.

An aspect of overall alignment is the need to align applications with their underlying support structures. Development environments traditionally have their own computer aided software engineering tools (CASE) that, for example, offer the means to specify requirements, draw design diagrams or generate applications. They also have a location for storage and for managing the elements that are created

After the design stage, the application must be further developed. Both the application and the environment must be prepared for the launch. *Application development* includes consistent coding conventions, guidelines and checklists, business-ready testing, setting up the organization of the development team. Deliverables of application development include scripts for starting and stopping an application or for monitoring hardware- and software configurations, SLA objectives and requirements, operational requirements and documentation, and support requirements.

4.13 Organization

Well performing organizations can quickly and accurately make the right decisions and execute them successfully. In order to achieve this, it is crucial that the roles (and responsibilities) are clearly defined. Amongst others, the roles include:
- process owner
- service design manager
- service catalogue manager
- service level manager
- availability manager
- security manager.

4.14 Methods, techniques and tools

It is extremely important to ensure that the tools to be used support the processes and not the other way around. There are various tools and techniques that can be used for supporting the service and component designs. Not only do they make the hardware and software designs possible, but they also enable the development of environment designs, process designs and data designs. Tools help ensure that service design processes function effectively. They enhance efficiency and provide valuable management information on the identification of possible weak points.

4.15 Implementation and operation

In this section the implementation considerations for service design are addressed:
- *Business impact analysis (BIA)* – BIA is a valuable source of information for establishing the customer's needs, and the

impact and risk of a service (for the business). The BIA is an essential element in the business continuity process and dictates the strategy to be followed for risk reduction and recovery after a catastrophe.

- *Implementation of service design* – Process, policy and architecture for the design of IT services, must be documented and used in order to design and implement appropriate IT services. In principle, they all should be implemented because all processes are related and often depend on each other. In this way you will get the best benefit. It is important do this in a structured way.
- *Prerequisites for success (PFS)* – Prerequisites are often requirements from other processes. For example, before service level management (SLM) can design the service level agreement (SLA), a service catalogue with customer-facing services and supporting services is necessary.

KPIs for the service design process include:
- Accuracy of the SLAs, OLAs and UCs.
- Percentage of specifications of the requirements of service design produced within budget.
- Percentage of service design packages (SDPs) produced on time.

Examples of challenges that are faced during implementation include:
- The need for synchronization of existing architecture, strategy and policy.
- The use of diverse technologies and applications instead of single platforms.
- Unclear or changing customer requirements.

There are several risks during the service design stage, including:
- maturity – if the maturity of one process is low, it is impossible to reach a high level of maturity in other processes
- unclear business requirements
- too little time allotted for service design.

Figure 4.9 shows that the output from every stage becomes an input to another stage in the lifecycle. Thus service strategy provides important input to service design, which in turn, provides input to the transition stage. The service portfolio provides information to every process in every stage of the lifecycle.

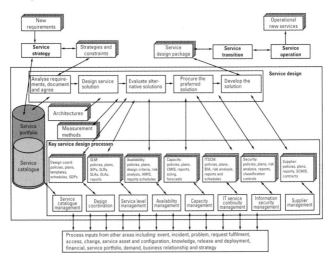

Figure 4.9 The most important relationships, inputs and outputs of service design
Source: the Cabinet Office

5 Lifecycle stage: service transition

5.1 Introduction

Service transition consists of the management and coordination of the processes, systems and functions required for the building, testing and deployment of new and changed services. Service transition establishes the services as specified in the service design stage, based on the customer and stakeholder requirements.

A service transition is effective and efficient if the transition delivers what the business requested within the limitations in terms of money and other necessary resources, as determined in the design stage.

An effective service transition ensures that the new or changed services are better aligned with the customer's business operation. For example: the capacity of the business to react quickly and adequately to changes in the market.

5.2 Basic concepts

The following *policies* are important for an effective service transition and apply to every organization. The approach does need to be adjusted to the conditions that are appropriate for each different organization:

- Define and implement guidelines and procedures for service transition.
- Implement all changes through service transition.
- Use common frameworks and standards.
- Re-use existing processes and systems.

- Coordinate service transition plans with the needs of the business.
- Create relations with stakeholders and maintain these.
- Set up effective controls on assets, responsibilities and activities.
- Deliver systems for knowledge transfer and decision support.
- Plan packages for releases and deployment.
- Anticipate and manage changes in plans.
- Manage the resources proactively.
- Continue to ensure the involvement of stakeholders at an early stage in the service lifecycle.
- Assure the quality of a new or changed service.
- Proactively improve service quality during a service transition.

5.3   Processes and other activities

A service transition generally comprises the following steps:
- planning and preparation
- building
- service testing and pilots
- planning and preparation of the deployment
- deployment, transition or retirement
- review and closing of service transition.

This section explains the processes and activities of a service transition.

Service transition processes:
- *Transition planning and support* – Ensures the planning and coordination of resources in order to realize the specification of the service design.

- *Change management* – Ensures that changes are implemented in a controlled manner, i.e. that they are evaluated, prioritized, planned, tested, implemented, and documented.
- *Service asset and configuration management (SACM)* – Manages the service assets and configuration items (CIs) in order to support the other service management processes.
- *Release and deployment management* – Aimed at the building, testing and deploying of the services specified in the service design, and ensures that the client can utilize the service effectively.
- *Service validation and testing* – Tests ensure that the new or changed services are "fit for purpose" and "fit for use".
- *Change evaluation* – Aimed at ensuring that each important point in the lifecycle of a significant change is properly evaluated. This evaluation is required for the authorization to proceed to the next step, for example before build and test, or before deployment.
- *Knowledge management* – Improves the quality of decision-making (for management) by ensuring that reliable and safe information is available during the service lifecycle.

Service transition activities:
- *Communication* is central during every service transition.
- Significant change of a service may also mean a change of the organization. *Organizational change management* should address *the emotional change cycle* (shock, avoidance, external blame, self blame and acceptance), *culture and attitudes*.
- *Stakeholder management* is a crucial success factor in service transition. A stakeholder analysis can be made to find out what the requirements and interests of the stakeholders are,

and what their final influence and power will be during the transition.

Change management, SACM and knowledge management influence and support all lifecycle stages. Release and deployment management, service validation and testing, and change evaluation are strongly focused at the service transition stage.

5.4 Transition planning and support

Introduction
Transition planning and support ensures the planning and coordination of resources in order to realize the specification of the service design. Transition planning and support plans changes and ensures that issues and risks are managed.

Basic concepts
The *service design package (SDP)* that was created in the service design stage contains all aspects of an IT service and its requirements through each stage of its lifecycle. It includes the information about the execution of activities of the service transition team.

A *release* should be defined, in which the following subjects are addressed:
- naming conventions, distinguishing release types
- roles and responsibilities
- release frequency
- acceptance criteria for the various transition stages
- the criteria for leaving early life support (ELS).

The following types of release can be defined:
- *Major release* – Important deployment of new hardware and software with, in most cases, a considerable expansion of the functionality.
- *Minor release* – These usually contain a number of smaller improvements; some of these improvements were previously implemented as quick fixes but are now included integrally within a release.
- *Emergency release* – Usually implemented as a temporary solution for a problem or known error.

Activities
The activities for planning are:
1. *Set up transition strategy* – The transition strategy defines the global approach to service transition and the assignment of resources.
2. *Prepare service transition* – The preparation consists of analysis and acceptance of input from other service lifecycle stages and other inputs; identifying, filing and planning RFCs; monitoring the baseline and transition readiness.
3. *Plan and coordinate service transition* – An individual service transition plan describes the tasks and activities required to deploy a release in a test and production environment.
4. *Support* – Service transition advises and supports all stakeholders. The planning and support team will provide insight for the stakeholders regarding service transition processes and supporting systems and tools.

Finally, service transition activities are monitored: the implementation of activities is compared with the way they were intended.

5.5   Change management

Introduction

The primary objective of change management is to enable beneficial changes to be made, with minimal disruption to IT services. Change management ensures that changes are deployed in a controlled way, i.e. they are evaluated, prioritized, planned, tested, implemented and documented.

Changes are made for proactive or reactive reasons. Examples of proactive reasons are cost reduction and service improvement. Examples of reactive reasons for change are solving service disruptions and adapting the service to a changing environment.

The change management process must:
- use standardized methods and procedures
- record all changes in the CMS
- take account of risks for the business.

Change management is not responsible for coordinating all of the service management processes to ensure the smooth implementation of projects. This activity is carried out by transition planning and support.

Basic concepts

A *request for change (RFC)* is a formal request to change one or more CIs. Complex changes may be preceded by a *change proposal*, which is usually created by the service portfolio management process (see "Key concepts" section with definitions).

Three types of change request are distinguished: a normal change, a standard change, and an emergency change. A *normal change* is the addition, modification or elimination of anything that could have an effect on IT services. The scope should include changes to all architectures, processes, tools, metrics and documentation as well as changes to IT services and individual configuration items.

A *standard change* is a pre-approved, low risk and relatively common change. Standard changes must be registered by change management. Each standard change should have a *change model*, specifying in detail how the change should be handled. A change model includes the steps to be taken, the chronological order of these steps, the responsibilities for the steps and activities, the timescales and thresholds, and the escalation procedures. Tools can be used to automate the handling of change models.

An *emergency change* is a change that must be introduced as soon as possible. For example, to repair a failure as soon as possible in an IT service that has a large negative impact on the business. An emergency change may have different authorization and may be documented after it has been completed.

Changes are often *categorized* as major, significant and minor, depending on the level of cost and risk involved, and on the scope and relationship to other changes.

The *priority of the change* is based on impact and urgency. Change management schedules the changes on the change calendar: the change schedule (CS).

The *change advisory board (CAB)* is a consultative body that regularly meets to help the change manager/change authority assess, prioritize and schedule the changes. In case of emergency changes, it can be necessary to identify a smaller group to make emergency decisions: the *Emergency CAB (ECAB)*.

No change should be approved without having a *fallback situation (remediation planning)* available.

A *post-implementation review (PIR)* should be carried out to determine if the change was successful and to identify opportunities for improvement.

Activities

The specific activities (see Figure 5.1) to manage individual changes are:

1. *Create and record the RFC* – An individual or department may submit an RFC. All RFCs are registered and must be identifiable.
2. *Review the RFC* – After registration, the stakeholders verify whether the RFC is illogical, unfeasible, unnecessary or incomplete, or whether it has already been submitted earlier.
3. *Assess and evaluate the change* – Based on the impact, risk assessment, potential benefits and costs of the change, and the business justification, the change authority determines whether a change is taken forward or not and who is concerned. The support of *change evaluation* may be required here.
4. *Authorize the change build and test* – For every change there is a formal authorization required, before the change is built and tested. This may be done by a role, person or group of people. This decision is communicated to the involved parties.

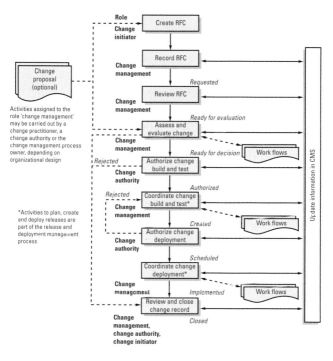

Figure 5.1 Change management
Source: the Cabinet Office

5. *Coordinate change build and test* – Authorized changes are passed to the relevant technical groups for building the changes. For changes that are part of a planned release, this may be controlled by the release and deployment management process.

6. *Authorize change deployment* – The change authority requires proof that the result of the change was properly built and tested. This may require a formal report.

7. *Coordinate change deployment* – This is part of the release and deployment management process. Remediation procedures should be prepared and documented in advance. For simple changes that are not part of a release, the change management process will coordinate this activity.

8. *Review and close change record* – Deployed changes are evaluated after some time (*post-implementation review (PIR)*). If the change is successful, its administration can be finalized (including the SKMS) and it can be closed.

5.6   Service asset and configuration management

Introduction

Service asset and configuration management (SACM) manages the service assets and configuration items (CIs) in order to support the other service management processes. SACM defines the service and infrastructure components and maintains accurate configuration records.

Basic concepts

A *service asset* is any resource or capability of a service provider.

A *configuration item (CI)* is any component or other service asset that is (or will be) managed in order to deliver an IT service.

An *attribute* is a piece of information about a CI. For example version number, name, location et cetera.

A *relationship* is a link between two CIs that identifies a dependency or connection between them. Relationships show how CIs work together to provide a service.

By maintaining relations between CIs a *logical model* of the services, assets and infrastructure is created. This provides valuable information for other processes.

A *configuration structure* shows the relations and hierarchy between CIs that comprise a configuration.

A *snapshot* ("moment in time", "footprint") is the state of a configuration at a certain point in time (for instance when it was inventoried by a discovery tool). It can be recorded in the CMS to remain as a fixed historical record of the configuration, not necessarily authorized.

Configuration management ensures that all CIs are provided with a *baseline* and that they are maintained. A baseline is a snapshot that is used as a reference point. Many snapshots may be taken and recorded over time but only some will be used as baselines. A baseline can be used to restore the IT infrastructure to a known configuration if a change or release fails.

CIs are *classified* (the act of assigning a category to a CI) to help manage and trace them throughout their lifecycles, for instance: service, hardware, software, documentation, personnel.

A *configuration management database* (CMDB) is a database used to store configuration records of CIs. A *configuration record* contains details of a CI. One or more CMDBs can be part of a configuration management system (CMS, Figure 5.2).

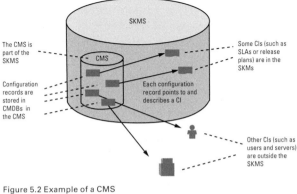

Figure 5.2 Example of a CMS
Source: the Cabinet Office

In order to manage large and complex IT services and infrastructures SACM needs to use a supporting system: the *configuration management system (CMS)*.

Various *libraries* are defined:
- A *secure library* is a collection of software and electronic CIs (documents) of a known type and status, with limited access.
- A *secure store* is a secure location where IT assets are stored.

The *definitive media library (DML)* is a secure store where the definitive, authorized (approved) versions of all media CIs are stored and monitored.

Definitive spares are spare components and assemblies that are maintained at the same level as the comparative systems within the live environment.

Software asset management (SAM) is the process responsible for tracking and reporting the use and ownership of software assets throughout their lifecycle. SAM is part of the overall SACM.

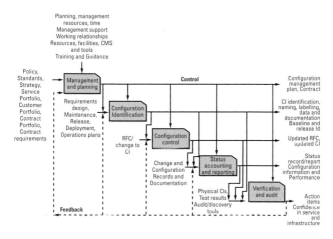

Figure 5.3 Service asset and configuration management
Source: the Cabinet Office

Activities

The basic SACM process activities (Figure 5.3) consist of:

1. *Management and planning* – The management team and configuration management decide what level of configuration management is needed and how this level will be achieved. This is documented in a configuration management plan.

2. *Configuration identification* – Configuration identification focuses on establishing a CI classification system. Configuration identification determines: the configuration structures and selection of CIs; the naming conventions of CIs, the CI labels; relations between CIs, the relevant attributes of CIs, type of CIs et cetera.

3. *Configuration control* – Configuration control ensures that the CIs are adequately controlled. No CIs can be added, adapted, replaced or removed without following the agreed procedure.
4. *Status accounting and reporting* – The lifecycle of a component is classified into different stages. For example: development or draft, approved and withdrawn. The stages that different types of CIs go through must be properly documented and the status of each CI must be tracked.
5. *Verification and audit* – SACM conducts audits to ensure that there are no discrepancies between the documented baselines and the actual situation; and that release and configuration documentation is present before the release is deployed.

5.7 Release and deployment management

Introduction
Release and deployment management is aimed at building, testing and delivering the capability to provide the services specified by service design.

Although release and deployment management is responsible for ensuring that appropriate testing takes place, the actual testing is carried out as part of the service validation and testing process. Release and deployment management is not responsible for authorizing changes, and requires authorization from change management at various stages in the lifecycle of a release.

Basic concepts
A *release* is one or more changes to an IT service that are built, tested and deployed together. A single release may include changes to hardware, software, documentation, processes and other components.

A *release unit* is a part of the service or infrastructure that is included in a release, in accordance with the organization's release guidelines.

A *release package* is a single release unit or (structured) collection of release units that will be built, tested and deployed together as a single release. All the elements of which the service consists – the infrastructure, hardware, software, applications, documentation, knowledge, et cetera – must be taken into account.

In the *release design* different considerations apply in respect of the way in which the release is deployed. The most frequently occurring options for the deployment of releases are: big bang versus phased, push and pull, automated or manual.

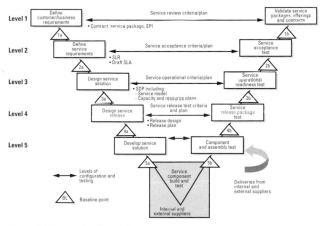

Figure 5.4 The service V model
Source: the Cabinet Office

The *V model* (Figure 5.4) is a convenient tool for mapping out the different configuration levels at which building and testing must take place. The left side of the V in this example starts with service specifications and ends with the detailed service design. The right side of the V reflects the test activities, by means of which the specifications on the left-hand side must be validated. In the middle we find the test and validation criteria (See 5.8 Service validation and testing).

Activities

The process activities of release and deployment management are:

1. *Release and deployment planning* – Prior to a deployment into production different plans are formulated. The type and number depends on the size and complexity of the environment and the changed or new service. Before approval can be given for the building and test phase, the service and release design is compared against the specifications of the new or changed service (validation). Logistics and delivery plans should be prepared. Pilots may be part of the chosen approach. This phase is under the control of change management authorization.

2. *Release build and test* – The release package is built, tested and checked into the DML. The building and test phase of the release consists of the management of general (common) infrastructure and services; use of release and building documentation; acquisition, purchasing and testing of CIs and components for the release; compilation of the release (release packaging); structuring and controlling the test environments. Test management is responsible for the coordination of the test activities and the planning and control of the implementation. The extent to which each deployment

team is prepared for the deployment (readiness assessment) is tested. This phase is under the control of change management authorization.

3. *Deployment* – The release package in the DML is deployed to the live environment. The following activities are important during deployment: the transfer of financial assets; transfer and transition of business and organization; transfer of service management resources; transfer of the service; deployment of the service; retirement of services; removal of superfluous assets. When all the deployment activities have been completed it is important to verify that all stakeholders are able to use the service as intended. This phase is under the control of change management authorization and ends with handover to the service operation functions and early life support. Early life support (ELS) is intended to offer extra support after the deployment of a new or changed service.

4. *Review and close* – In the review of a deployment, check whether the knowledge transfer and training were adequate; all user experiences have been documented; all fixes and changes are complete and all problems, known errors and workarounds have been documented; the quality criteria have been complied with.

5.8   Service validation and testing

Introduction
Testing of services during the service transition stage ensures that the new or changed services are *fit for purpose (utility)* and *fit for use (warranty)*.

The goal of service validation and testing (Figure 5.5) is to ensure the delivery of the added value that is agreed and expected.

When not properly tested, additional incidents, problems and costs will occur.

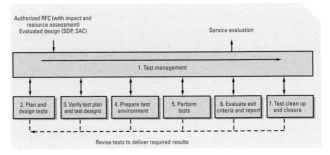

Figure 5.5 Service validation and testing
Source: the Cabinet Office

Basic concepts

The *service model* describes the structure and dynamics of a service provided by service operation. The structure consists of main and supporting services and service assets. When a new or changed service is designed, developed and built, these service assets are tested in relation to design specifications and requirements. Activities, flow of resources, coordination, and interactions describe the dynamics.

The *test strategy* defines the entire testing approach and the allocation of required resources.

A *test model* consists of a test plan, the object to be tested and test scripts which indicate the method by which each element must be tested.

The service design package (SDP) defines entry and exit criteria for all test perspectives.

By using *test models*, such as a *V model* (see Figure 5.4), testing becomes a part of the service lifecycle early in the process.

Fit for purpose means that the service does what the client expects of it, so that the service supports the business. *Fit for use* addresses such aspects as availability, continuity, capacity and security of the service.

In addition to all kinds of functional and non-functional *test types*, *role playing* is also possible based on perspective (target group).

Activities
The following test activities can be distinguished:
- *Validation and test management* – Test management consists of planning and managing (control), and reporting on the activities taking place during all test stages of the service transition.
- *Planning and design* – Test planning and design activities take place early in the service lifecycle and relate to resources, supporting services, planning milestones and delivery and acceptance.
- *Verification of test plan and design* – Test plans and designs are verified to make sure that everything (including scripts) is complete, and that test models sufficiently take into account the risk profile of the service in question, and all possible interfaces.
- *Preparation of the test environment* – Prepare the test environment and make a baseline of the test environment.
- *Testing* – The tests are executed using manual or automated testing techniques and procedures. Testers register all results.

- *Evaluate exit criteria and report* – The actual results are compared with projected results (exit criteria).
- *Clean up and closure* – Make sure that the test environment is cleaned. Evaluate the test approach and determine issues that need improvement.

5.9 Change evaluation

Introduction
The change evaluation process provides the means of determining the performance of a service change in the context of likely impacts on business outcomes, and on existing and proposed services and IT infrastructure. The actual performance of a change is assessed against its predicted performance. Risks and issues related to the change are identified and managed. Change evaluation delivers important input for continual service improvement (CSI) and future improvement of service development and change management (Figure 5.6).

Basic concepts
A *change evaluation report* contains a risk profile, a deviations report, a qualification and validation statement (if necessary), and a recommendation (to accept or refuse the change).

The *predicted performance* of a service is the expected performance. The *actual performance* is the performance following a service change.

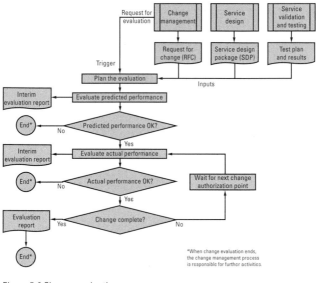

Figure 5.6 Change evaluation
Source: the Cabinet Office

Activities

The evaluation process consists of the following activities:

1. *Planning the change evaluation* – When planning a change evaluation, the intended and unintended effects of a change are analyzed.

2. *Evaluating the predicted performance* – Perform a risk assessment based on the customer's specifications, the predicted performance and the performance model. Send an interim assessment report to change management if the change evaluation shows that the predicted performance represents an unacceptable risk to the change or deviates from the acceptance criteria. Cease the change evaluation activities while awaiting a decision from change management.

3. *Evaluating the actual performance* – After implementation of the service change, service operation reports on the actual performance of the service. Perform a second risk assessment, again based on the customer's specifications, the predicted performance and the performance model. Send a new interim assessment report to change management if the change evaluation shows that the actual performance represents an unacceptable risk and cease the change evaluation activities while awaiting a decision from change management.

Send a change evaluation report to change management if the evaluation is approved.

5.10 Knowledge management

Introduction
Knowledge management improves the quality of decision-making by ensuring that reliable and safe information is available during the service lifecycle.

Effective sharing of knowledge requires the development and maintenance of a service knowledge management system (SKMS, Figure 5.7)). This system should be available to all information stakeholders and suit all information requirements.

Basic concepts
Knowledge management is often visualized using the *DIKW* structure: Data-Information-Knowledge-Wisdom. Quantitative data from metrics are transformed into qualitative information. By combining information with experience, context, interpretation and reflection it becomes knowledge. Ultimately,

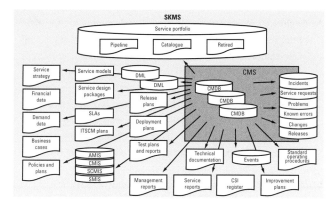

Figure 5.7 The service knowledge management system
Source: the Cabinet Office

knowledge can be used to make the right decisions which comes down to wisdom.

The basis of the *service knowledge management system (SKMS)* is formed by a considerable amount of data in one or more configuration management databases (CMDBs) which are part of the configuration management system (CMS). The CMS provides input for the SKMS and consequently supports the decision-making process. However, the scope of the SKMS is broader. Information is also stored that relates to matters such as:

- the experience and skills of staff
- information about peripheral issues such as the behavior of users and the performance of the organization
- requirements and expectations of suppliers and partners.

There are a number of knowledge transfer techniques, such as learning styles; knowledge visualization; driving behavior; seminars; advertisements; newsletter, newspaper.

Activities

Knowledge management consists of the following activities, methods and techniques:

1. *Knowledge management strategy* – An organization needs an overall knowledge management strategy. If such a strategy is already in place, the service management knowledge strategy can link into it. The knowledge management strategy also focuses specifically on identifying and documenting relevant knowledge, and on the data and information that support this knowledge.

2. *Knowledge transfer* – The transfer of knowledge is a challenging task that requires, in the first place, an analysis to determine what the knowledge gap is between the department or person in possession of the knowledge and those in need of the knowledge. Based on the outcome of this analysis, a communication (improvement) plan is formulated to facilitate the knowledge transfer.

3. *Managing data, information, and knowledge* – Data and information management consists of the following activities: establishing data and information requirements; defining the information architecture; establishing data and information management procedures; evaluation and improvement.

4. *Use of the SKMS* – Supplying services to customers in different time zones and regions and with different operating hours imposes strenuous requirements on the sharing of knowledge. For this reason the supplier must develop and maintain an SKMS system that is available to all stakeholders and suits all information requirements.

5.11 Organization

Service transition is actively managed by a *service transition manager*. The service transition manager is responsible for the daily management and control of the service transition teams and their activities.

Generic roles are:
- *Process owner* – ensures that all process activities are carried out.
- *Service owner* – has the responsibility, toward the client, for the initiation, transition and maintenance of a service.

Other roles that can be distinguished within service transition include:
- service asset manager
- configuration manager
- change manager
- deployment manager
- configuration analyst
- configuration management system manager
- risk-evaluation manager
- service knowledge manager.

Responsibility areas include:
- test support
- early life support
- building and test environment management
- change advisory board (CAB)
- configuration management team.

5.12 Methods, techniques and tools

Technology plays an important part in the support of service transition. It can be divided into two types:
- *IT service management systems* – Such as enterprise frameworks which offer integration opportunities linking

with the CMS or other tools; system, network and application management tools; service dashboard and reporting tools.
- *Specific ITSM technology and tools* – Such as service knowledge management systems; collaboration tools; tools for measuring and reporting; test (management) tools; publishing tools; release and deployment technology.

5.13 Implementation and operation

The implementation of service transition in a "greenfield" situation (from zero) is only likely when establishing a new service provider. Most service providers therefore focus on the improvement of the existing service transition (processes and services). For the improvement of service transition the following five aspects are important:

1. *Justification* – Show the benefits in business terms of effective service transition to all stakeholders.
2. *Design* – Factors to take into account when designing are standards and guidelines, relationships with other supporting services, project and program management, resources, all stakeholders, budget and means.
3. *Introduction* – Do not apply the improved or newly implemented service transition to current projects.
4. *Cultural aspects* – Even formalizing existing procedures will lead to cultural changes in an organization. Take this into consideration.
5. *Risks and advantages* – Do not make any decisions about the introduction or improvement of service transition without an insight into the expected risks and advantages.

There is input/output of knowledge and experience from and to service transition. For example: service operation shares practical experiences with service transition as to how similar services behave in production. Also, experiences from service transition supply inputs for the assessment of the designs from service design. Like processes in a process model, all stages in a lifecycle will have outputs that are inputs in another stage of that lifecycle.

For a successful service transition, several challenges need to be conquered, such as:
- taking into account the needs of all stakeholders
- finding a balance between a stable operating environment and being able to respond to changing business requirements
- creating a culture which is responsive to cooperation and cultural changes
- ensuring that the quality of services corresponds to the quality of the business
- a clear definition of the roles and responsibilities.

Potential risks of service transition are:
- de-motivation of staff
- unforeseen expenses
- excessive cost
- resistance to changes
- lack of knowledge sharing
- poor integration between processes
- lack of maturity and integration of systems and tools.

6 Lifecycle stage: service operation

6.1 Introduction

Service operation involves coordinating and carrying out activities and processes required to provide and manage services for business users and customers within a specified agreed service level. Service operation is also responsible for management of the technology required to provide and support the services.

Service operation is an essential stage of the service lifecycle. If the day-to day operation of processes is not properly conducted, controlled and managed, then well-designed and well-implemented processes will be of little value. In addition there will be no service improvements if day-to-day activities to monitor performance, assess metrics and gather data are not systematically conducted during service operation.

6.2 Basic concepts

Service operation is responsible for the fulfillment of processes that optimize the service costs and quality in the service management lifecycle. As part of the organization, service operation must help ensure that the customer (business) achieves their goals. Additionally, it is responsible for the effective functioning of components supporting the service.

Achieving balance in service operation:
- Handling conflict between maintaining the current situations and reacting to changes in the business and technical environment. Service operation must try to achieve a balance between these conflicting priorities.

- Achieving an IT organization in which stability and response are in balance. On the one hand, service operation must ensure that the IT infrastructure is stable and available. At the same time, service operation must recognize the business needs change and must embrace change as a normal activity.
- Achieving an optimal balance between cost and quality. This addresses IT's challenge to continually improve the quality of services while at the same time reducing or at the very least maintaining costs.
- Achieving a proper balance in reactive and proactive behavior. A reactive organization does nothing until an external stimulus forces it to act. A proactive organization always looks for new opportunities to improve the current situation. Usually, proactive behavior is viewed positively, because it enables the organization to keep a competitive advantage in a changing environment. An over-proactive attitude can be very costly, and can result in distracted staff.

It is very important that the service operation staff are involved in service design and service transition, and, if necessary, in service strategy. This will improve the continuity between business requirements, technology design and operation by ensuring that operational aspects have been given thorough consideration.

Communication is essential. IT teams and departments, as well as users, internal customers and service operation teams, have to communicate effectively with each other. Good communication can prevent problems.

6.3 Processes and other activities

This section explains the processes and activities of service operation. There are some key service operation processes that must link together to provide an effective overall IT support structure.

Service operation processes:

- *Event management* – Surveys all events that occur in the IT infrastructure in order to monitor the regular performance, this can be automated to trace and escalate unforeseen circumstances.
- *Incident management* – Focuses on restoring failures of services as quickly as possible for customers, so that these have a minimal impact on the business.
- *Request fulfillment* – The process of dealing with service requests from the users, providing a request channel, information, and fulfillment of the request.
- *Problem management* – Includes all activities needed for a diagnosis of the underlying cause of incidents, and to determine a resolution for those problems.
- *Access management* – The process of allowing authorized users access to a service, while access of unauthorized users is prevented.

Service operation common activities:

- *Monitoring and control* – Based on a continual cycle of monitoring, reporting and undertaking action. This cycle is crucial to providing, supporting and improving services.
- *IT operations* – Fulfill the day-to-day operational activities that are needed to manage the IT infrastructure.
- There are a number of operational activities which ensure that the technology matches the service and process goals,

including *server and mainframe management and support, network management, storage and archive, database administration, directory services management, desktop and mobile device support, middleware management,* and *Internet/ web management.*

- *Facilities and data centre management* refers to management of the physical environment of IT operations, usually located in computing centers or computer rooms. Facility management comprises for example building management, equipment hosting, power management and shipping and receiving.

6.4   Event management

Introduction

An *event* is defined as "A change of state that has significance for the management of an IT service or other configuration item." The term is also used to mean an alert or notification created by any IT service, CI or monitoring tool. Events typically require IT operation personnel to take actions, and often lead to incidents being logged.

Event management is the process that monitors all events that occur through the IT infrastructure to allow for normal operation and also to detect and escalate exceptional conditions. Event management can be automated to trace and escalate unforeseen event circumstances.

Basic concepts

Events may be classified as:
- *Events that indicate a normal operation* – For example a user logging on to use an application.

- *Events that indicate an abnormal operation* – For example a user who is trying to log on to an application with an incorrect password or a PC scan that reveals the installation of unauthorized software.
- *Events that signal an unusual but not exceptional operation* – It may provide an indication that the situation requires a little more supervision. For example utilization of a server's memory reaches within five per cent of its highest acceptable level.

Event management can be applied to any service management aspect that must be managed and can be automated.

Activities

The main activities of the event management process are:

1. *An event occurs* – Events occur all the time, but not all of them are detected or registered. Therefore, it is important to understand what event types must be detected.
2. *Event notification* – Most CIs are designed in such a way that they communicate specific information about themselves in one of the following ways:
   - A management tool probes a device and collects specific data (this is also called "polling").
   - The CI generates a report if certain conditions are met.
3. *Event detection* – A management tool or agent detects an event report and reads and interprets it.
4. *Event logging* – An event and subsequent actions are logged as an event record in the event management tool, or it can simply be left as an entry in the system log of the device or application that generated the event.
5. *First-level event correlation and filtering* – Event filtering decides whether or not the event is communicated to a

management tool. If ignored, the event will usually be recorded in a log file on the device, but no further action will be taken. This is normally performed by an automated agent.

6. *The significance of events* – The event is categorized according to its significance, for example using the categories *informational*, *warning*, and *exception*.

7. *Second-level event correlation* – The meaning of the event is determined, often based on a set of business rules to determine the business impact.

8. *Further action required?* – If the event is recognized, a response is required. The mechanism that initiates that response is called a trigger.

9. *Response selection* – The response is selected from a variety of options, including auto response, alert and human intervention, submitting an RFC, opening an incident record, open or link to a problem record.

10. *Review actions* – All important events or exceptions should be checked to determine whether they have been treated correctly, or whether event types are counted.

11. *Closing the event* – The event is closed. Some events remain open until specific actions have been taken.

The diagram in Figure 6.1 reflects the flow of event management.

Each event type is able to trigger event management. Among other things, triggers include:

- Exceptions at every level of CI performance established in the design specifications, operational level agreements or standard processing procedures.
- An exception in a business process that is monitored by event management.
- A status change that is found in a device or database record.

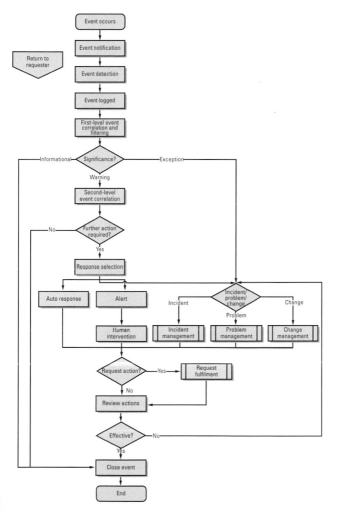

Figure 6.1 Event management
Source: the Cabinet Office

6.5   Incident management

Introduction

The incident management process handles all incidents. These may be failures, faults or bugs that are reported by users (generally via a call to the service desk) or technical staff, or that are automatically detected and reported by monitoring tools.

An incident can be defined as: "an unplanned interruption to an IT service or reduction in the quality of an IT service. Failure of a CI that has not yet affected service is also an incident."

The purpose of incident management is to restore *normal service operation* as quickly as possible and minimize the adverse impact on business operations, thus ensuring that agreed levels of service quality are maintained. 'Normal service operation' is defined as an operational state where services and CIs are performing within their agreed service and operational levels.

Basic concepts

In incident management, the following elements should be taken into account:
- *Timescales* – Agree on time limits for all stages and use them as targets in OLAs and UCs.
- *Incident models* – An incident model is a way of pre-defining the steps that are necessary to handle a process (in this case, the processing of certain incident types) in an agreed way. Usage of incident models helps to ensure that standard incidents will be handled correctly and within the agreed timeframes.

- *Impact* – The effect of an incident upon business processes.
- *Urgency* – A measure of how long it will be before the incident will have a significant impact on business processes.
- *Priority* – A category for the relative importance of an incident, based on impact and urgency.
- *Major incidents* – A major incident is an incident for which the degree of impact on the user community is extreme. Major incidents require a separate procedure, with shorter timeframes and higher urgency. Agree on what defines a major incident and map the entire incident priority system.

People sometimes confuse a major incident with a problem. However, an incident always remains an incident. Its impact or priority may increase, but it never becomes a problem. A problem is the underlying cause of one or more incidents and always remains a separate entity.

Activities

The incident management process consists of the following steps (Figure 6.2):

1. *Identification* – The incident is detected or reported.
2. *Logging* – An incident record is created.
3. *Categorization* – The incident is coded by type, status, impact, urgency, SLA, et cetera.
4. *Prioritization* – Every incident gets an appropriate prioritization code to determine how the incident is handled by support tools and support staff. For example 1-5, where "1" is critical and "5" is planned.
5. *Initial diagnosis* – A diagnosis is carried out to try to discover the full symptoms of the incident. Incident data are compared against other incidents, problems and known errors, to enable incident matching for quicker resolution.

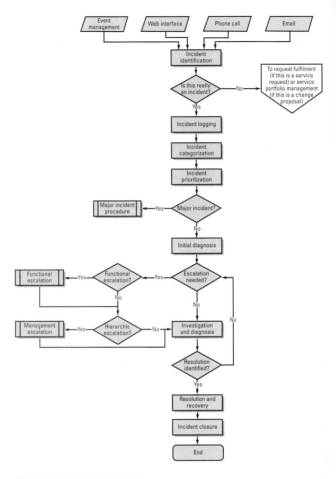

Figure 6.2 Incident management
Source: the Cabinet Office

6. *Escalation* – When the service desk cannot resolve the incident, the incident is escalated for further support (*functional escalation*). If incidents are more serious, the appropriate IT managers must be notified (*hierarchic escalation*).
7. *Investigation and diagnosis* – If there is no known solution, the incident is investigated.
8. *Resolution and recovery* – Once the solution has been found, the issue can be resolved.
9. *Closure* – The service desk should check that the incident is fully resolved and that the user is satisfied with the solution and the incident can be closed.

Rules for re-opening of incidents should be agreed, but predefined rules (like time thresholds) might be set to limit this to a relatively short period right after closing the incident.

6.6   Request fulfillment

Introduction

The term service request is used as a general description for the various requests that users submit to the IT department. A service request is a request from a user for information, advice, a standard change, or access to a service.

For example, a service request can be a request for a password change or the additional installation of a software application on a certain work station. Because these requests occur on a regular basis and involve little risk, it is better that they are handled in a separate process.

Basic concepts

Many service requests recur on a regular basis, enabling the development of predefined *request models*. This is why a process flow can be devised in advance, stipulating the stages needed to handle the requests, the individuals or support groups, time limits and escalation paths involved. The service request is usually handled as a *standard change*.

Submitting service requests is often supported by self-help practices, where users can submit their own service request through menu selection with a link to service management tools.

Like all other call types, service requests should be tracked throughout their lifecycle to support proper handling and reporting on their status. This requires a registration system, where service request records are described throughout their lifecycle. Statuses may include draft, in review, suspended, waiting authorization, rejected, cancelled, in progress, completed, and closed.

Handling service requests appropriately also requires that they are prioritized, for instance using a standard set of criteria based on impact and urgency.

In conflicting situations, it may be necessary to escalate requests. Escalation paths should be predefined in appropriate request models.

Service requests involve cost, and should therefore be financially approved. The cost of standardized service requests may be predefined, e.g. in the SLA. Billing or cross-charging may also be included. Other constraints may also require approval before the service request is handled.

Like other operational call types, service requests can be handled by the service desk, or routed to a second or higher line, leaving the service desk in charge of monitoring the progress of request handling.

Before being closed, a service request should be checked, to see if all policies have been met.

Activities

Request fulfillment (Figure 6.3) consists of the following activities:

1. *Receive request* – The process should start with a formalized request that can be registered and maintained. The request can come from a wide variety of sources.
2. *Request logging and validation* – Whatever source the request came from, it should now be logged with all required details, including a unique number, category, impact, urgency, requestor information, authorization, etc, comparable to the information required for an incident or RFC.
3. *Request categorization* – The request type should be categorized to enable its processing as well as providing management information. Categories might be based on the service that is involved, the activity type, the request type, the function involved, or the CI type.
4. *Request prioritization* – The request priority is determined by weighing impact and urgency, comparable to the way this is done in the incident management process.
5. *Request authorization* – Each request requires appropriate authorization, before being processed. If not properly

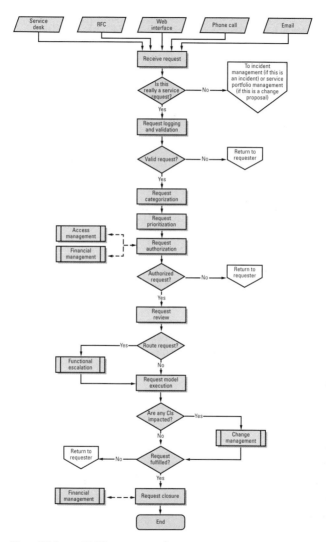

Figure 6.3 Request fulfillment process flow
Source: the Cabinet Office

authorized, the request should be returned to the requester, with proper explanation.

6. *Request review* – Once approved, the request must be given to the function that will fulfill it. This often is the service desk that received the request, but in other cases it will be routed to second line functions.

7. *Request model execution* – Executing the service request in a repeatable and consistent way is stimulated by using request models.

8. *Request closure* – Control of the request fulfillment resides with the service desk, just like in incident management. The service desk makes sure that the request indeed has been fulfilled, that all administration was done as required, that the requester is informed and satisfied with the delivery, and that the request record is then formally closed.

Rules for re-opening of service requests should be agreed, but predefined rules (like time thresholds) might be set to limit this to a relatively short period right after closing the request.

6.7 Problem management

Introduction

A *problem* is defined as: "the unknown cause of one or more incidents."

Problem management is responsible for the control of the lifecycle of all problems. The primary objective of problem management is to prevent problems and incidents, eliminate repeating incidents, and minimize the impact of incidents that cannot be prevented.

Basic concepts

Problems should be administered in a separate management system, apart from incidents.

A *root cause* of an incident is the fault in the service component that made the incident occur.

A *workaround* is a way of reducing or eliminating the impact of an incident or problem for which a full resolution is not yet available.

A *known error* is a problem that has a documented root cause and a workaround. If a new application, system or release contains faults that cannot be resolved before going live, these are registered as known errors.

In addition to creating a *known error database (KEDB)* for faster diagnosis, the creation of a *problem model* for the handling of future problems may be useful. This standard model supports the steps that need to be taken, the responsibilities of people involved and the necessary timescales.

Problem management (Figure 6.4) has both reactive and proactive aspects:

- *Reactive problem management* – Analyzing and resolving problems in response to one or more incidents. Reactive problem management is performed by service operation.
- *Proactive problem management* – Identifying and solving problems and known errors before further incidents related to them can occur. Proactive problem management includes the identification of trends or potential weaknesses. It is initiated by service operation, but usually driven by CSI.

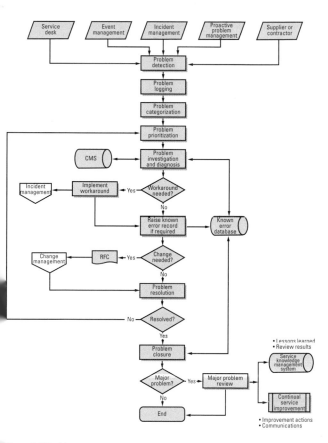

Figure 6.4 Problem management
Source: the Cabinet Office

Activities

Problem management (Figure 6.4) has the following activities:
- *Problem detection* – Reactive or proactive detection is possible, for example through a study of the cause of a major incident or through regular inspection of incident data.
- *Problem logging* – All problems should be administered with enough detail to support the process and later matching activities.
- *Problem categorization* – Problems should be categorized in the same way as incidents, preferably with the same system of categories.
- *Problem prioritization* – Problems should be prioritized the same way as incidents, using the same reasons and preferably with the same system of priority codes.
- *Problem investigation and diagnosis* – The problem needs to be investigated to try to diagnose the root cause of the problem. Available techniques include chronological analysis, Kepner & Tregoe, brainstorming, hypothesis testing, technical observation post, Ishikawa diagrams, and Pareto analysis.
- *Workarounds?* – Sometimes it is possible to find a workaround to overcome the difficulties. The problem record remains open and the process continues to look for a definitive solution.
- *Raising a known error record* – When the root cause and a workaround have been determined and documented, a known error record is raised and associated with the problem record. The known error is registered in the known error database (KEDB).
- *Problem resolution* – When a resolution has been determined for the root cause, the problem should be resolved, most likely through a change.
- *Problem closure* – After final resolution of the problem, the problem record and any associated open incident record can

be closed, after completing the documentation. The status of any related known error record should be updated to show that the resolution has been applied.
- *Major problem review* – Following closure of a major problem, a review should be promptly conducted, to look for lessons learned.

6.8   Access management

Introduction
Access management grants authorized users the right to use a service, and denies unauthorized users access. Some organizations also call it "rights management" or "identity management".

Access management can be initiated via a number of mechanisms, for example by means of a *service request* with the service desk.

Basic concepts
Access management has the following basic concepts:
- *Access* – Refers to the level and scope of the functionality of services or data that a user is allowed to use. This is guided and directed by information security policies.
- *Identity* – Refers to the information about the people who the organization distinguishes as individuals; establishes their status in the organization.
- *Rights* – Rights are also called privileges. Refers to the actual settings for a user; the service (group) they are allowed to use. Typical rights include reading, writing, executing, editing and deleting.

- *Services or service groups* – Most users have access to multiple services; it is therefore more effective to grant every user or group of users access to an entire series of services that they are allowed to use simultaneously.
- *Directory services* – Refers to a specific type of tool used to manage access and rights.

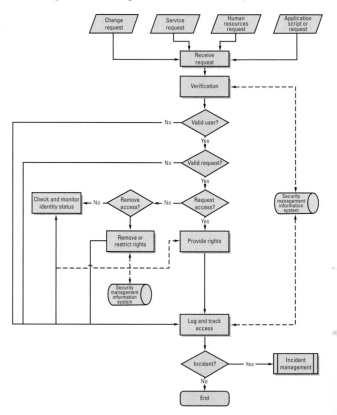

Figure 6.5 Access management process flow
Source: the Cabinet Office

Activities

Access management consists of the following activities:

- *Request access* – Access (or limitation of access) can be requested via a number of mechanisms, such as a standard request generated by the human resources department; a request for change (RFC), an RFC submitted via the request fulfillment process, execution of an authorized script or option.
- *Verification* – Access management must verify every access request for an IT service from two perspectives:
  - Are the users requesting access, really the persons they say they are?
  - Do the users have a legitimate reason to use the service?
- *Provide rights* – Give verified users access to IT services. Access management does not decide who gets access to what IT services; it only executes the policy and rules defined by service strategy and service design.
- *Check and monitor identity status* – Access management does not only respond to requests; it must also ensure that the rights it has granted are used correctly. User roles may vary over time. Changes like job changes, promotion, dismissal, retirement all influence their service needs.
- *Log and track access* – This is why access monitoring and control must be included in the monitoring activities of all technical and application management functions as well as in all the service operation processes.
- *Remove or restrict rights* – In addition to granting rights to use a service, access management is also responsible for withdrawing those rights; but it cannot make the actual decision.

6.9   Common service operation activities

Apart from the five operation processes, there are a number of operational activities that ensure that technology is aligned with the overall service and process objectives. Usually, these activities are rather technical, supporting the operational day-to-day delivery of IT services.

Monitoring and Control

The measuring and control of services is based on a continuous cycle of monitoring, reporting and initiating action. This cycle is essential to the supply, support and improvement of services and also provides a basis for setting strategy, designing and testing services, and achieving meaningful improvement.

Three terms play a leading role in monitoring and control:
- *Monitoring* – Refers to the observation of a situation to discover changes that occur over time.
- *Reporting* – Refers to the analysis, production and distribution of the outputs of the activity that is being monitored.
- *Control* – Refers to the management of the usefulness or behavior of a device, system or service. There are three conditions:
  - The action must ensure that the behavior conforms to a defined standard or norm.
  - The conditions leading to the action must be defined, understood and confirmed.
  - The action must be defined, approved and suitable for these conditions.

There are two levels of monitoring:
- *Internal monitoring and control* – Focuses on activities and items that exist within a team or department. For instance

a service desk manager may monitor the number of calls to determine how many members of staff are needed to answer the telephone.
- *External monitoring and control* – Although each team or department is responsible for managing its own area, they do not act independently. Each team or department will also be controlling items and activities on behalf of other groups, processes or functions. For example, the server management team monitors the CPU performance on important servers and keeps the workload under control. This allows essential applications to perform within the target values set by application management.

The best-known model for the description of control is the monitor control loop. Although it is a simple model, it has many complex applications in IT service management. Figure 6.6 reflects the basic principles of control. *Open loop systems* perform activities regardless of environmental conditions, while *closed loop systems* respond to environmental changes.

The monitoring/control loop concept can be used to manage:
- the performance of activities in a process or procedure
- the effectiveness of the process or procedure as a whole
- the performance of a device or a series of devices.

There are different types of monitoring tools, whereby the situation determines which type of monitoring is used:
- active versus passive monitoring
- reactive versus proactive monitoring
- continuous measuring versus exception-based measuring
- performance versus outputs.

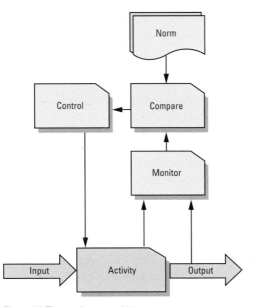

Figure 6.6 The monitor control loop
Source: the Cabinet Office

ITIL does not define the inputs/outputs for monitoring and control in detail. In general, anything could be monitored. However, the main issue here is the definition of monitoring and control objectives. The definition of monitoring and control objectives should ideally start with the definition of the service level requirements documents. The service design process will help to identify the inputs for defining operational monitoring and control norms and mechanisms.

Monitoring without control is irrelevant and ineffective. Monitoring must always be aimed at achieving the service and operational objectives. Therefore, if there is no clear reason for the monitoring of a system or service, there should be no monitoring.

IT operations

To focus on delivering the service as agreed with the customer, the service provider will first have to manage the technical infrastructure that is used to deliver the services. Even when no new customers are added and no new services have to be introduced, no incidents occur in existing services, and no changes have to be made in existing services – the IT organization will be busy with a range of service operation. These activities focus on actually delivering the agreed service.

The *operations bridge* is a central point of coordination that manages various events and routine operational activities, and reports on the status or performance of technological components.

An operations bridge brings together all vital observation points in the IT infrastructure so that they can be monitored and managed with minimum effort in a central location.

The operations bridge combines many activities, such as console management, event handling, first line network management, and support outside office hours. In some organizations, the service desk is part of the operations bridge.

In *job scheduling*, IT operations execute standard routines, queries or reports that technical and application management teams have handed over as part of the service or as part of daily routine maintenance tasks.

Essentially, *backup and restore* is a component of good continuity planning. Service design must therefore ensure that there are proper backup strategies for every service. Service transition must ensure that they are properly tested. An organization must protect its data, which includes backup and storage of data in reserved protected (and if necessary, accessible) locations.

A complete backup strategy must be agreed with the business and must cover the following elements:
- What data should the backup include, and how often must it be made?
- How many generations of data must be retained?
- The backup type and the checkpoints that are used.
- The locations used for storage and the rotation schedule.
- Transport methods that are used.
- Required tests that are used.
- Planned recovery point; the point to which data must be recovered after an IT service resumes.
- Planned recovery time; the maximum allowed time to resume an IT service after an interruption.
- How will it be checked that the backups are functional when they need to be restored?

In all cases, the IT operations staff must be qualified in backup and restore procedures. These procedures must be documented properly in the procedure manual of IT operations. Where necessary, you should include specific requirements or targets in OLAs or UCs, and specify user or customer obligations and activities in the relevant SLA.

A *restore* can be initiated from several sources, varying from an event indicating data corruption to a service request from a user or customer. A restore may be necessary in case of:

- corrupt data
- lost data
- a disaster recovery plan / IT service continuity situation
- historical data required for forensic investigation.

Print and output management

Many services provide their information in *print* or electronic form (*output*). The service provider must ensure that the information ends up in the right place, in the right way and in the right form. This often involves Information security.

Laws and regulations may play an important part in print and output. The archiving of important or sensitive data is particularly important.

Service providers are generally deemed to be responsible for maintaining the infrastructure to make the print and output available to the customer (printers, storage). In this case, that task must be set in the SLA.

Server and mainframe management and support

Servers and mainframes are essential components of an IT infrastructure, and require proper management. The involved activities are similar for both component types. The activities include operating system support, license management, third-level incident support, procurement advice, system security, managing virtual servers, capacity and performance management, and other routine activities.

Network management
Connectivity, provided through networks, is essential to service delivery. Network management is responsible for all network management, and for liaising with third-party network suppliers. Activities include planning, installing and managing networks and network operating systems, third-level support, network monitoring, network security, and network administration.

Storage and archive
The ever-growing volume of data requires proper management through storage and archive. Activities include design and management of all storage devices and storage networks, setting up storage and archiving policies, data storage and retrieval, and third-line support.

Database administration
Database administration works closely with application management functions. Activities include developing and managing database policies, designing and managing databases, database monitoring, and third-level support.

Directory services management
A directory service is an application that manages information about the resources available on a network. It is used for access management. Activities include developing directory policies, directory administration, rights management, directory monitoring, and third-level support.

Desktop and mobile device support
Workstations are essential to a user, and types may vary more and more, especially in the mobile environment. Desktop and mobile device support activities include policy development,

designing and managing standard workstation images, and third-level support for all involved processes.

Middleware management
Middleware is software that connects two or more software components or applications, and is often used in architectures like service-oriented architectures (SOAs). Middleware management is involved with all relevant management activities to ensure the agreed functioning of middleware infrastructure.

Internet/web management
Organizations and IT infrastructures are normally heavily dependent upon internet access and websites. Internet and web management teams may be installed to fulfill all management activities related to internet and website infrastructure.

Facilities and data centre management
Facilities management is the function responsible for managing the physical environment where the IT infrastructure is located – for example, power and cooling, building management, access management, and environmental monitoring. Requirements for data centres are already addressed in service design. Data centres are highly concentrated facilities that require integrated management to be able to support the service operation. Activities involved relate to all management activities that require the availability and functioning of data centres and related facilities.

6.10 Organization

Service operation has some logical *functions* that deal with service desk, technical management, IT operations management and application management:

- A *service desk* is the single point of contact (SPOC) for users, dealing with incidents, change requests and service requests.
- *Technical management* refers to the groups, departments or teams that provide technical expertise and overall management of the IT infrastructure.
- *IT operations management* executes the daily operational activities needed to manage the IT infrastructure, according to the performance standards defined during service design.
- *Application management* is responsible for managing applications in their lifecycle.

Roles and responsibilities within service operation include:
- service desk manager
- service desk supervisor
- service desk analysts
- super users
- technical managers/team leaders
- technical analysts/architects
- technical operators
- IT operations manager
- shift leader
- IT operations analysts
- IT operators
- application managers and team leaders
- application analysts and architects
- incident manager
- problem manager
- contract manager
- building manager.

There are several ways to organize service operation functions, and each organization will come to its own decisions based on its size, geography, culture and business environment.

Service desk

A service desk is a functional unit with staff involved in differing service events. These service events come in by phone, internet or infrastructure, events which are reported automatically.

The service desk is a vitally important element of the IT department of an organization. It must be the only contact point, the single point of contact (SPOC), for IT users and it deals with all incidents, access requests and service requests. The staff often uses software tools to record and manage all events.

The primary purpose of the service desk is to restore "normal service" to users as quickly as possible. "Normal service" refers to what has been defined in the SLAs. This may be resolving a technical error, but also filling a service request or answering a question.

There are many ways to organize a service desk. The most important options are:

- *Local service desk* – The local service desk is located at or physically close to the users it is supporting.
- *Centralized service desk* – The number of service desks can be reduced by installing them at one single location.
- *Virtual service desk* – By using technology, specifically the internet, and by the use of support tools, it is possible to create the impression of a centralized service desk, whereas the associates are in fact spread out over a number of geographic or structural locations.
- *Follow the sun* – Two or more service desks are located in different continents and combined in order to offer a 24/7 service.

- *Specialized service desk groups* – Incidents relating to a specific IT service may be routed straight to the specialized group.

Besides resuming normal service to the user as quickly as possible there are specific responsibilities for a service desk, for example:
- logging all incident/service request details
- providing first-line investigation and diagnosis
- resolving incidents/service request
- escalating incidents/service requests a service desk cannot resolve themselves within agreed timescales
- informing users about the progress
- closing all resolved incidents, requests and other calls
- updating the CMS under the direction and approval of configuration management if so agreed.

In order to evaluate the performance of the service desk at regular time intervals, *metrics* must be established. This way, the maturity, efficiency, effectiveness and potentials can be established and the service desk actions improved.

Besides following "hard" metrics in the performance of the service desk, it is also important to use "soft" metrics: the client and user satisfaction surveys (for example do clients and users find that their phone calls are properly answered? Was the service desk associate friendly and professional?). Users can best complete this type of metrics, but specific questions about the service desk itself may also be asked.

Technical management
Technical management plays a dual role. It is the custodian of technical knowledge and expertise related to managing

the infrastructure. But it also provides the actual resources to support the ITSM lifecycle.

Generic technical management activities include the identification, documentation, development, and recruiting of skills that are required to manage and operate the IT infrastructure and to deliver IT services. Generic activities also include the participation in all IT management processes, such as design and development, change and release deployment, risk assessment, testing, supplier management, event management, incident and problem resolution, and any other activity requiring the specific skills of technical management staff.

Technical management may be organized in various ways, e.g. according to infrastructure domains (mainframe team, desktop team, network team), according to platforms (web team, UNIX team, SAP team), according to geography (office, location, country), or any other mechanism for the optimization of skills availability.

IT operations management

IT operations management has two functions: *IT operations control*, which ensures that routine operational tasks are carried out to deliver agreed IT services, and *facilities management*, for the management of physical IT environment, usually data centres or computer rooms.

IT operations control oversees all operational activities and IT infrastructure events. This can be done with the help of an *operations bridge* or *network operations centre*. IT operations control is responsible for tasks including console management, job scheduling, backup and restore, print and output management, and performance and maintenance activities. In many cases, staff from technical and application management groups form part of the IT operations management function.

IT operations management is responsible for documentation like standard operating procedures (SOPs), operation logs, shift schedules and reports, and operations schedules.

Application management
Application management also plays an important role in the design, testing and improvement of applications that are part of IT services. One of the key decisions in application management is build-or-buy: whether to buy an application that supports the required functionality, or whether to build the application in-house according to the organization's requirements. Contrary to *application development*, which is mainly concerned with the one-time activities for requirements, design and build of applications, *application management* covers the entire ongoing lifecycle of an application, from *requirements*, *design* and *build*, through *deploy* and *operate*, up to *optimize*. This means that application management will support each stage of the IT service lifecycle, and will be actively supporting the execution of all relevant processes. For this purpose application management also is responsible for documentation including application portfolio, application requirements, use cases, designs and manuals.

6.11 Methods, techniques and tools
An important requirement for service operation is an integrated IT service management technology (or toolset) with the following core functionality:
- self-help (e.g. FAQ's on a web interface)
- workflow or process management engine
- an integrated configuration management system (CMS)

- technology for detection, implementation and licenses
- remote control
- diagnostic utilities
- reporting capabilities
- dashboards
- integration with business service management.

6.12 Implementation and operation

There are some general implementation guidelines for service operation:

- *Managing changes in service operation* – Service operation staff must implement changes without negative impact on the stability of offered IT services.
- *Service operation and project management* – There is a tendency not to use project management processes when they would in fact be appropriate. For example, major infrastructure upgrades, or the deployment of new procedures are significant tasks where project management can be used to improve control and manage costs and resources.
- *Determining and managing risks in service operation* – In a number of cases, it is necessary that risk evaluation is conducted swiftly, in order to take appropriate action. This is especially necessary for potential changes or known errors, but also in case of failures, projects, environmental risks, suppliers, security risks and new clients that need support.
- *Operational staff in service design and transition* – Service operation staff should be particularly involved in the early stages of service design and transition. This will ensure that the new services will actually work in practice and that they can be supported by service operation staff.
- *Planning and implementation of service management technologies* – There are several factors that organizations

must plan before and during implementation of ITSM support tools, such as licenses, implementation, capacity checks and timing of technology/implementation.

For a successful service operation, several challenges need to be overcome, such as:
- Lack of involvement among development and project staff.
- Justifying the financing.
- Managing ineffective service transition, the use of virtual teams and the balance between internal and external relationships.

There are some critical success factors:
- management support
- defining champions
- business support
- hiring and retaining staff
- service management training
- appropriate tools
- test validity
- measuring and reporting.

Risks to successful service operation include:
- insufficient financing and resources
- loss of momentum in implementation service operation
- loss of important staff
- resistance to change
- lack of management support
- suspicion of service management by both IT and the business
- changing expectations of the customer.

7 Lifecycle stage: continual service improvement

7.1 Introduction

IT departments must continually improve their services in order to remain appealing to the business. This is placed within the lifecycle stage of continual service improvement (CSI). In this stage, measuring and analyzing are essential in identifying the services that are profitable and those that need to improve.

CSI should be applied throughout the entire service lifecycle, in all stages from service strategy to service operation. This way, it becomes an inherent part of both developing and delivering IT services.

CSI mainly measures and monitors the following matters:
- *Process compliance* – Are the new or modified processes being followed?
- *Quality* – Do the various process activities meet their goals?
- *Performance* – How efficient is the process?
- *Business value of a process* – Does the process make a difference?

7.2 Basic concepts

A *CSI manager* should be accountable for managing all CSI issues, but responsibility for specific service improvements should reside with the *service owner*.

Like in other processes, a register should be kept to record all improvement initiatives. This *CSI register* is part of the service knowledge management system (SKMS) and should follow best practices like the ones available in other lifecycle stages and processes, with categorization, prioritization, authorization, et cetera.

Drivers for improvements can either be internal or external. Internal aspects include organizational structures, culture, new knowledge and technologies, et cetera. External aspects include regulation, legislation, competition, external customer requirements, market pressures and economics. The SLM process is a key principle of CSI, enabling service improvement to be effectively aligned with business interest. Knowledge management also plays a key role in CSI.

Organizational change is needed to make continual improvement a permanent part of the organizational culture. John P. Kotter, Professor of Leadership at the Harvard Business School, discovered eight crucial steps to successful organizational change:

- create a sense of urgency
- form a leading coalition
- create a vision
- communicate the vision
- empower others to act on the vision
- plan for and create quick wins
- consolidate improvements and create more change
- institutionalize the changes.

In the 1930s, the American statistician Deming developed a step-by-step improvement approach: the *Plan-Do-Check-Act Cycle (PDCA)*:
- *Plan* – What needs to happen, who will do what and how?
- *Do* – Execute the planned activities.
- *Check* – Check whether the activities yield the desired result.
- *Act* – Adjust the plan in accordance to the checks.

These steps are followed by a consolidation stage to engrain the changes into the organization. The cycle is also known as the Deming Cycle (Figure 7.1).

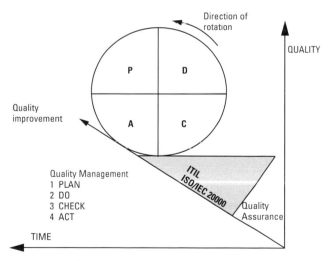

Figure 7.1 PDCA Cycle

CSI uses the PDCA Cycle in two areas:
- *Implementation of CSI* – Plan, implement (do), monitor, measure, and evaluate (check) and adjust (act) CSI.

- *Continual improvement of services and processes* – This area focuses on the "check" and "act" stage, with few activities in the "plan" and "do" stage, such as setting goals.

Service measurement is a crucial element of each improvement initiative. To enable improvement measurement, *baselines* should be available as starting points for later comparison. Baselines should be documented, recognized and accepted throughout the organization. An important concept that builds on service measurement is the CSI seven-step improvement process (see Section 7.4).

A *metric* measures whether a certain variable meets its set target. CSI needs three types:
- *technology metrics* – performance and availability of components and applications
- *process metrics* – performance of service management processes
- *service metrics* – end service results, measured by component metrics.

Define *critical success factors (CSFs)*: elements essential to achieving the business mission. KPIs following from these CSFs determine the quality, performance, value, and process compliance. They can either be *qualitative* (e.g. customer satisfaction surveys), or *quantitative* (e.g. costs of a printer incident).

Metrics supply quantitative *data*. CSI transforms these into qualitative *information*. Combined with experience, context, interpretation and reflection this becomes *knowledge*. The seven-step improvement process focuses on the acquirement of *wisdom*:

being able to make the correct assessments and the correct decisions by using the data, information and knowledge in the best possible way. This is called the *data-information-knowledge-wisdom* model (DIKW).

Governance drives organizations and controls them. *Corporate governance* provides good, honest, transparent and responsible management of an organization. *Business governance* results in good company performances. Together they are known as *enterprise governance*. See Figure 7.2. *IT governance* is part of enterprise governance and comprises both corporate governance and business governance.

CSI policies capture agreements about measuring, reporting, CSFs, KPIs and evaluations.

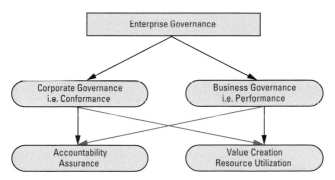

Figure 7.2 The enterprise governance framework (Source: CIMA)

7.3 Processes and other activities

This section explains the processes and activities of continual service improvement.

Continual service improvement works across the service lifecycle and involves many activities. These have been pulled together into a single contiguous process: *the seven-step improvement process.*

Before you start with an improvement process, you should set the direction, using the CSI approach (6 phases):

1. *What is the vision?* – Formulate a vision, mission, goals and objectives together with the business.
2. *Where are we now?* – Record the current situation and set the baseline.
3. *Where do we want to be?* – Determine measurable targets.
4. *How do we get there?* – Draw up a detailed service improvement plan (SIP).
5. *Did we get there?* – Measure whether the objectives have been achieved, and check whether the processes are complied with.
6. *How do we keep the momentum going?* – Engrain the changes in order to maintain them.

7.4 Seven-step improvement process

Introduction

The *seven-step improvement process* describes how to measure and report on service improvement. This process is closely aligned to the PDCA Cycle and the CSI approach, which should result in a *service improvement plan (SIP)*. Figure 7.3 shows how the PDCA Cycle and the seven-step improvement process mesh together.

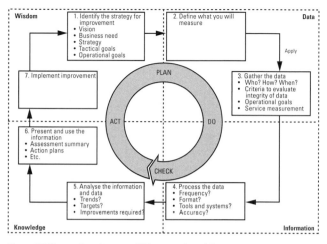

Figure 7.3 Connections between CSI approach and the seven-step
improvement process
Source: the Cabinet Office

Basic concepts

Measuring is critical in CSI. It is step 3 of the seven-step
improvement process as discussed below. It should, however,
never become a goal unto itself. Always keep in mind *why* you
measure.

Before an organization can produce meaningful measurements, it
needs to set its *baseline*, by answering the question "where are we
now?". If there is little data available, first determine a baseline
of relevant data.

Each management level should be addressed in the measuring
process: strategic goals and objectives, tactical process maturity
and operational metrics and KPIs. This way, a *knowledge spiral*

develops: the information from step 6 (Present and use the information) in an operational cycle is input for step 3 (Gather the data) in a tactical cycle, and information from step 6 at the tactical level will provide data to step 3 of a cycle at the strategic level.

Activities

CSI measures and processes measurements in a continual improvement process in seven steps:

- *Step 1: Identify the strategy for improvement* – This must follow from the vision (phase 1 of the CSI approach) and precede the assessment of the current situation (phase 2 of the CSI approach).
- *Step 2: Define what you will measure* – This step follows from phase 3 of the CSI approach: where do we want to be? By researching what the organization can measure, it will discover new business requirements and new IT options. By using a gap analysis CSI can find areas for improvement and plan these (phase 4 of the CSI approach).
- *Step 3: Gather the data (measure)* – In order to verify whether the organization has reached its goal (phase 5 of the CSI approach), it must perform measurements following from its vision, mission, goals and objectives.
- *Step 4: Process the data* – The processing of data is to determine the right presentation format appropriate to each audience.
- *Step 5: Analyze the information and data* – Discrepancies, trends and possible explanations are prepared for presentation to the business (phase 5 of the CSI approach).
- *Step 6: Present and use information* – The stakeholder is informed whether the goals have been achieved (still phase 5).

- *Step 7: Implement improvement* – Create improvements, establish a new baseline and start the cycle from step 1.

The cycle is preceded and closed by identification of vision and goals, which returns in phase 1 of the CSI approach: determine the vision.

The seven-step improvement process and the Deming cycle are aligned as follows:
- *Plan*
  1. dentify the strategy for improvement
  2. Define what you will measure
- *Do*
  3. Gather the data
  4. Process the data
- *Check*
  5. Analyze the information and data
  6. Present and use the information
- *Act*
  7. Implement improvement.

The inputs for the seven-step improvement process going into step 1 consist of:
- service level requirements
- service catalogue
- vision, mission, goals and objectives of the organization and its units
- governance requirements
- budget
- balanced scorecard
- results from SIP coming from step 7.

The *output* of step 1 is a list of what should be measured, serving as *input* for step 2. A list of what can be measured is the *output* of step 2. These two lists provide input for step 3, which creates the following *output*:
- monitoring plan and procedures
- collected data concerning the ability by IT to meet business expectations
- agreement on the reliability and applicability of data.

Step 4 processes this into reports and logically grouped data ready for analysis as an *input* for step 5. *Output* from step 5 is information turned into knowledge, according to the DIKW model. step 6, must translate knowledge into wisdom which is required to make strategic, tactical and operational decisions.

The *input*s for step 7 are improvement opportunities suggested from step 6. Step 7 assesses which opportunities provide the best possible outcome and implements those opportunities. This results in an SIP, which is the *output* of step 7. Measure whether desired improvements have delivered what you expected and use it as new *input* for step 1.

7.5 Organization

Besides temporary roles such as project managers, CSI describes the following generic roles:
- CSI manager
- service knowledge manager
- service owner
- process owner
- process manager
- process practitioner
- reporting analyst.

7.6   Methods, techniques and tools

Service measurement, including the determination of *baselines*, and using *metrics*, is an important enabler for service improvement. There are various other methods and techniques to check whether planned improvements actually produce measurable improvements:

- *Effort and cost* – Improvement initiatives require a business case to consider their cost-effectiveness.
- *Return on investment (ROI)* – Measuring the result of the cost spent on improvement initiatives is an important technique to support investment decisions and to develop business cases.
- *Implementation review and evaluation* – Evaluates whether the improvements produce the desired effects.
- *Assessments* – Compares the performance of a process or organization against a performance standard, such as an SLA or a maturity standard.
- *Benchmarking* – A special type of assessment: organizations compare (parts of) their processes with the performance of the same types of processes that are commonly recognized as "best practice".
- *Gap analysis* – Determines where the organization is now and the size of the gap with where it wants to be.
- *Balanced scorecard* – Includes four different perspectives on organizational performance: customer, internal processes, learning and growth and financial.
- *SWOT-analysis* – Looks at the strengths, weaknesses, opportunities and threats of an organization or component.
- *Rummler-Brache swim-lane diagram* – Visualizes the relationships between processes and organizations or departments with "swim lanes". Swim lanes are strong tools for communication with business managers, as they describe a

process from an organizational viewpoint, and this is the way most managers look at a process.

In most cases, one method or technique is not enough: try to find the best mix for your organization.

CSI needs different types of software to support, test, monitor and report on the ITSM processes. The requirements for enhancing tools need to be established and documented in the answer to the question: 'Where do we want to be?'

Service reporting reports on the results achieved and on the developments in service levels. The aim is to convincingly support with facts any added value IT will have for the business. IT should agree with the business on the layout, contents and frequency of the reports.

A *reporting framework* is a policy that is formulated according to the rules by which you report. It should be established together with the business and service design, per business unit, so you can distinguish between, for example, production and sales departments. Once this has been determined, data can be translated automatically (if possible) into meaningful reports. The reporting framework should at least contain:
- target groups and their view of the services delivered
- agreement as to what should be measured and what to report
- defining all terms and upper and lower limits
- basis for all calculations
- report planning
- access to reports and media used
- meetings to discuss the reports.

In order to provide useful reports to a customer, these reports should be set up from a business and end-to-end perspective. A customer is not interested in details about the functioning of the technical infrastructure through which services are provided, but only in the service itself.

Service reporting distinguishes the following generic activities:
- *Gather data* – First, determine the goal and target group of the report and consider how the report is going to be used.
- *Process and apply data* – Create a hierarchical overview of the performance over the past period, focusing on events that may impact the business performance. Describe how the IT department is going to combat those threats. Also describe what went well and how IT provides value to the business.
- *Publish the information* – Publish information for the different stakeholders at all levels of the organization. Use marketing and communication techniques to reach the different target groups such as the business and IT management.
- *Tune the reporting to the business* – Consider by data group if it is valuable for the target group. Look at this from an end-to-end perspective.

Evaluate continually whether the existing reporting provides clear and unambiguous information about the performance of the IT department, and adjust your reporting if this is no longer the case.

The *inputs* for service reporting are the data gathered in step 3 of the seven-step improvement process. It is important to determine what the *outputs* should look like well before the inputs arrives. IT departments frequently gather large amounts of data, which are not all equally interesting to the business. Start, therefore, by determining the goal and target group of the report and consider how the report is going to be used. Is management going to read it, can managers and department heads consult it online or are you going to present the results at a meeting? What will be done with it next?

Consider your audience. The organizational level of the target group will also influence its interest for different sorts of output:

1. *Strategic thinkers* – Strategic thinkers want short reports, with lots of attention to the risks, organization image, profitability and cost savings.
2. *Directors* – Directors want more detailed reports which summarize the development measured in time, indicating how processes support the company goals, and warning of risks.
3. *Managers and supervisors* – Managers and supervisors deal with observing the goals, team and process performance, distribution of resources and improvement initiatives. Measurements and reports must indicate how the process results are contributing to this.
4. *Team leaders and staff* – Team leaders and staff will look to emphasize the individual contribution to the company result; focus should be to fix individual metrics, acknowledge their skills and consider which training potential is available in order to involve them in the processes.

7.7   Implementation and operation

Before you implement CSI you must establish:
- roles for trend analysis, reporting and decision-making
- a testing and reporting system with the appropriate technology

- services are evaluated internally before the IT organization discusses the test results with the business.

The *business case* must clarify whether it is useful to start with CSI. On the basis of a set *baseline* an organization can compare the *benefits* and *costs* of the present situation with the benefits and costs of the improvement. Costs may be related to labor, training and tools.

Benefits of CSI may be:
- shorter time to market
- customer bonding
- lower maintenance costs.

Critical success factors for CSI include:
- adoption by the whole organization, including the senior management
- clear criteria for the prioritization of improvement projects
- technology to support improvement activities.

Introduction of CSI comes with the following challenges and risks:
- too little knowledge of the IT impact on the business and its important processes
- neglecting the information from reports
- insufficient resources, budget and time
- trying to change everything at once
- resistance against (cultural) changes
- poor supplier management
- lack of sufficient testing of all improvement aspects (people, process and products).

CSI uses a lot of data from the entire service lifecycle and virtually all its processes. CSI thus gains insight into the improvement opportunities of an organization.

Service level management, from the design stage of the lifecycle, is the most important process for CSI. It agrees with the business what the IT organization needs to measure and what the results should be. SLM maintains and improves the quality of IT services by constantly agreeing, monitoring and reporting on IT service levels.

As with all other changes in the lifecycle, CSI changes must go through the change, release, and deployment process. CSI must therefore submit a *request for change* (RFC) with change management and conduct a *post implementation review* (PIR) after implementation. The CMDB should be updated as well.

Acronyms

AMIS	availability management information system
APMG	APM Group
BCM	business continuity management
BCP	business continuity plan
BCS	British Computer Society
BIA	business impact analysis
BPO	business process outsourcing
BRM	business relationship manager
BU	business unit
CAB	change advisory board
CASE	computer aided software engineering
CCM	component capacity management
CFIA	component failure impact analysis
CI	configuration item
CIO	chief information officer
CMDB	configuration management database
CMIS	capacity management information system
CMS	configuration management system
CS	change schedule
CSF	critical success factor
CSI	continual service improvement
DIKW	data information knowledge wisdom
DML	definitive media library
ECAB	emergency change advisory board
ELS	early life support
FTA	fault tree analysis
GTB	grow the business
HR	human resources
ISMS	information security management system
ITIL	Information Technology Infrastructure Library

ITSCM	IT service continuity management
itSMF	IT Service Management Forum
ITT	invitation to tender
KEDB	known error database
KPI	key performance indicator
KPO	knowledge process outsourcing
LCS	Loyalist Certification Services
M_o_R	Management of Risk
MTBF	mean time between failures
MTBSI	mean time between service incidents
MTTR	mean time to repair
MTRS	mean time to restore service
OGC	Office of Government Commerce
OLA	operational level agreement
PBA	pattern of business activity
PDCA	plan do check act
PFS	prerequisites for success
PIR	post-implementation review
PRINCE2	PRojects IN Controlled Environments
PSO	projected service outage
RACI	responsible, accountable, informed, consulted
RAD	rapid application development
RAG	red, amber, and green
RFC	request for change
ROI	return on investment
RTB	run the business
SAC	service acceptance criteria
SACM	service asset and configuration management
SAM	software asset management
SCM	service catalogue management
SCMIS	supplier and contract management information system

SDLC	service development lifecycle
SDP	service design package
SFA	service failure analysis
SFIA	Skills Framework for the Information Age
SIP	service improvement plan
SKMS	service knowledge management system
SLA	service level agreement
SLAM	SLA monitoring
SLM	service level management
SLR	service level requirement
SMS	service management system
SoC	separation of concerns
SoR	statement of requirement
SPI	service provider interface
SPM	service portfolio management
SPOC	single point of contact
SPOF	single point of failure
SWOT	strengths, weaknesses, opportunities and threats
TCU	total cost of utilization
TSO	The Stationary Office
TTB	transform the business
UC	underpinning contract
UP	user profile
VBF	vital business function
VCD	variable cost dynamics

References

Bon, J. van, (Ed.) (2007), *Foundations of ITIL V3*. Zaltbommel, Van Haren Publishing.

ITIL. *Service Design* (2011). OGC. London: TSO.

ITIL. *Service Operation* (2011). OGC. London: TSO.

ITIL. *Service Strategy* (2011). OGC. London: TSO.

ITIL. *Service Transition* (2011).OGC. London: TSO.

ITIL. *Continual Service Improvement* (2011). OGC. London: TSO.

ISO/IEC 20000

ISO/IEC 20000 - An Introduction
Promoting awareness of the certification for organizations within the IT Service Management environment.

English €49.95 excl tax

ISBN 978 90 8753 081 5 (english edition)

Implementing ISO/IEC 20000 Certification - The Roadmap
Practical advice, to assist readers through the requirements of the standard, the scoping, the project approach, the certification procedure and management of the certification.

English €39.95 excl tax

ISBN 978 90 8753 082 2 (english edition)

ISO/IEC 20000-1:2011 - A Pocket Guide
A quick and accessible guide to the fundamental requirements for corporate certification.

English €15.95 excl tax

ISBN 978 90 8753 682 4 (english edition)

www.vanharen.